CHICAGO
❧ CITY ON THE MOVE ❧

CHICAGO
❖ CITY ON THE MOVE ❖

 FEATURING **PHOTOGRAPHS** SELECTED FROM THE
ARCHIVES OF THE CHICAGO **TRANSIT** AUTHORITY

MICHAEL WILLIAMS
RICHARD CAHAN
and BRUCE MOFFAT

❖ FOREWORD BY ❖
STUART DYBEK

CHICAGO
CITYFILES PRESS
PUBLISHERS

2007

PUBLISHED BY CITYFILES PRESS, CHICAGO
E-MAIL: CITYFILESPRESS@RCN.COM
WEBSITE: CITYFILESPRESS.COM

ISBN: 0-9785450-3-6

FIRST EDITION

BOOK DESIGNED BY MICHAEL WILLIAMS AND RICHARD CAHAN

PRINTED IN CANADA BY FRIESENS

FRONTISPIECE: SOUTH BOULEVARD STATION, AT CHICAGO AVENUE AND SOUTH BOULEVARD IN EVANSTON, UNDER CONSTRUCTION IN 1929.

TABLE OF CONTENTS

FOREWORD STUART DYBEK

Contrary to songs on the subject, I never felt there was much magic to a bus. Especially a diesel-fume-spewing bus that one is trapped behind in traffic. A bus has to compete for its share of the street. That lack of privilege can make it late, especially in freezing, snowy weather when you most want it to be there on time.

Streetcars by comparison rode their own track. Neither photographs nor words can recapture their seared pneumatic smell, but I inhaled it with pleasure as I climbed aboard, and would welcome smelling it again. I'd welcome the feel of their straw seats. A musical *ding* punctuated its stops and starts, along with the occasional crackle of a blue spark from the trolley wire above. The first job I remember wanting as a child wasn't fireman, but streetcar conductor.

Back then—the "then" of remarkable conveyances, an aspect of the past that the photographs in this book somehow manage to evoke—the "L" seemed a streetcar in the sky above the street.

It still seems a remarkable conveyance to me. There's its overhead screech, like some bird of prey feeding on rush hour; there's the way it emerges from its tunnel, a crescendo of metallic wind propelled along a sparking third-rail that can fry you. I don't know if it is scientifically possible, but a drunken character in a story I wrote almost loses his life by taking a leak on the electric rail.

The girders that support the "L" flaunt their urban musculature in a way most skyscrapers are too modest to reveal. You can take its daily tour from slums to suburbs; you can ride it beneath the city. In a story I wrote called "Nighthawks," a conga-drumming Orpheus descends into that underworld. Composed of iron and shadow, the "L" can't help but throw a noirish mood, and photographing the "L" or writing about it becomes almost inescapably figurative. That's where the magic happens. For me, only Lake Shore Drive is as iconic as the Chicago "L." Both are about taking you somewhere.

The photos and text of *Chicago: City on the Move* powerfully capture not only the history, but that sense of mood and magic that makes history live. It's the rare kind of book that makes one viscerally aware that the present is a stop along a continuum of track we share with the city's past.

LOOKING NORTH ABOVE THE
ADAMS AND WABASH STATION
IN THE 1920S.

A Route to the Past

Hidden among thousands of file cabinets at the Chicago Transportation Authority are twenty-two special ones. They contain a remarkable archive of transportation images—more than 20,000 prints and 200,000 negatives carefully stored away.

Placed in chronological order, the photographs demonstrate how the early streetcars and rapid transit trains cut through the prairie and created Chicago's neighborhoods, guiding growth and guiding life. They show lines of track embedded in miles of roads. And they show big-riveted ribbons of iron that carried trains and giant dynamos that powered them.

They show a transportation system built by dreamers who had a steadfast belief in the city and in those who lived there.

What the sisters Carrie must have thought upon arriving in Chicago from their Midwestern farms. What a city of grace; what a city of beauty. Streetcars with cowcatchers to clear the tracks, elevated trains with opal shades and enamel handholds. These photographs tell that story—not just of the growth of a transit system, but the growth of the city.

The images in the archive were taken by the CTA and its predecessor agencies going back to the days when "street railroads" ran alongside automobiles on public corridors. The majority of the photos come from four sources: the Chicago Surface Lines, which operated the city's streetcars and trolley buses; the Chicago Rapid Transit Company, which ran elevated trains; the Chicago Motor Coach Company, which ran motor buses, and the CTA, which took over nearly all public transportation in Chicago in 1947. The images also come from prints dating back to the 1870s from five streetcar companies that later formed the Chicago Surface Lines and four rapid transit companies that formed the Chicago Rapid Transit Company.

Scattered in the files are a few photos from outside sources that were purchased for commercial reasons, and photos from most of the thirty-six transit companies that have operated in the city. Many of these early pictures were taken as memories by motormen and conductors, or by freelance photographers with their names penciled or stamped on the backs.

As you can see (nobody reads the text of a photo book before sneaking a peak at the pictures), the photographs show a gritty, sturdy, durable city—of factories and nightclubs, amusement parks and short-order restaurants. And they show a contingent of workers determined to make it possible for Chicagoans to get about their lives and take part in the city. They show a century of Chicago—a city on the move.

CTA PHOTOGRAPHER ART TONNER PERCHES ON THE LEDGE OF A LOOP SKYSCRAPER TO PHOTOGRAPH A GARFIELD PARK RAPID TRANSIT TRAIN TURNING ONTO WELLS STREET IN THE BLOCK BETWEEN JACKSON BOULEVARD AND VAN BUREN STREET IN 1955. HE WAS SHOWING THE NEW LOOP CONNECTION OF THE GARFIELD PARK LINE AFTER THE WELLS STREET TERMINAL WAS DEMOLISHED.

Over the decades, only a few hundred of these pictures have ever been seen—in Chicago history and transit books and the annual CTA calendar. The prints and negatives comprise one of the largest and most detailed collections of mass transit photographs in America. Nobody has been given the opportunity to study the entire collection and make sense of how these photos fit together until now.

Most of the photographers who created this collection are anonymous. They seldom received written credit, and left behind little but their work. Chicago's first full-time transit photographer was hired by the Chicago Surface Lines in 1914, the year the company was formed. Richard Millar's primary job was to take clear photographs of accidents that could be used for insurance purposes or in court to defend the company. "A witness speaking from memory may become a bit hazy about the relative positions of track, trolley pole and curb; but the camera does not forget," wrote the *Surface Service Magazine* about the company's decision to create a photo department.

All but a handful of the vintage accident pictures are long gone—tossed out several years after cases were settled. But photographs of equipment, known as rolling stock, and traffic conditions fill the files to this day. "No description of traffic congestion in the Loop can convey adequately an understanding of conditions that are instantly apparent from a glance at a good photograph. And a photograph makes a record that is not affected by time."

Photographer Millar was born in Scotland and received his photographic training there. After moving to the United States and joining the Surface Lines staff, he was particularly dedicated—working long hours, but leaving the company to volunteer as a photo instructor during the First World War. Like many photographers of that day, he was part scientist. "He lets no detail escape," wrote the company magazine. "He is a constant student of chemistry as applied to photographs and is normally not only up to all the technical wrinkles of his business but in many cases is fully two jumps ahead. Incidentally he finds the twenty-four hour day a trifle short of the time needed to enable him to keep up with his work and the two assistants who are associated with him often wonder when he sleeps or if he sleeps at all."

Millar was succeeded as the company's chief photographer in the late 1920s by Alfred R. "Fred" Chouinard, who came with quite a photo pedigree. Chouinard's father established one of Chicago's first photo studios, and Fred's first job was strapping his father's portrait subjects into a chair and clamping their heads so that they would stay still for long exposures. Fred became a professional photographer in 1897, and attached himself to the city's early movie industry. He shot and developed film for the old Essanay Studios and American Film Company, working with such silent film stars as Charlie Chaplin. Before coming to the Surface Lines, Chouinard also worked briefly with Walt Disney, helping him figure out how to animate his early cartoons after young Disney returned to his Chicago birthplace around 1917. Chouinard, with a cigar in his mouth and carrying satchels of film and equipment, was a fixture at the Surface Lines and at the CTA until his retirement in 1957.

The Surface Lines was much larger and more profitable than the Chicago Rapid Transit Company. The streetcar company employed a chief photographer and up to four assistants. The transit line's chief photographer was A. F. Scholz, who started in the early 1920s and continued through the late 1940s. The story goes that Scholz began his employment as an accountant and took up photography after his boss complained about the amount of money the company was spending on outside photographers. During the 1920s, Scholz recorded the construction of the Niles Center Line in the north sub-

PHOTOGRAPHERS JAM THE MONROE STREET STATION ON THE OPENING DAY OF MILWAUKEE-DEARBORN SUBWAY LINE IN 1951. COWBOY ACTOR MONTE BLUE JOINED MAYOR MARTIN KENNELLY AT THE CEREMONY.

urbs and the Westchester Line in the west suburbs. He developed a detailed procedure for making accident photographs—taking dozens of images only a few feet apart to demonstrate exactly how collisions occurred. He also took more than 200 photographs of the major streets that the elevated lines crossed. The accident photos and many of the intersection shots are gone from the files, but much of his work documenting the busiest years of the rapid transit company remains.

Scholz's work ledgers indicate that he may have lost full-time work status with the rapid transit company during the Depression (as did many workers), but he continued as a freelance photographer for the company and other Chicago firms. Engineer and amateur photographer Charles E. Keevil, whose transit station shots are highlighted later in the book, took photos that supplemented Scholz's work.

When the CTA took over the Chicago Surface Lines, Rapid Transit Company and later the Chicago Motor Coach Company, the photography department grew larger. As at the early companies, the primary function of the new CTA photo team was to make accident records and document equipment. During the 1950s, Chouinard led a team that included Ed Evenson, Thor Haanig, Addison Jones, Gar Francis and Art Tonner from CTA's headquarters in the Merchandise Mart. The staff was similar to that of a daily newspaper: photographers reported for work, were given assignments (called "specials") and returned with results. Most of the staff was on 24-hour call, ready to be dispatched to the scene of serious accidents. Days were devoted to photographing traffic flow, new equipment, or assignments to fill promotional pamphlets, route maps or the *Transit News*, the CTA's employee magazine.

The photography of Millar, Chouinard, Scholz and the later CTA photographers was industrial in nature. Photographers were meticulous—creating precise pho-

tos with written notes often printed right on the photo negatives they produced. Their priority was to accurately depict a scene. But they also created a wondrous record of the city. These photos make up the majority of this book. The quality of the work is exceptional—and irreplaceable. No other archive duplicates the work.

Unlike photographs taken by railfans, who were usually confined to the perimeter of a scene, these pictures were taken by photographers who could go wherever they wanted—on the subway tracks, in the middle of intersections on lift trucks, behind the police lines at accident scenes, or even balanced on the ledge of a highrise buildings in the Loop.

They produced extraordinary images even when that was not their intention. In 1963, photographer Gar Francis, who first worked as a Chicago Motor Coach driver, was assigned to photograph the Howard Street Station before it was remodeled. The point of this assignment was to document the need for change at these old stations—to supply a "before" to accompany the "after" shots to come. The pictures show an old interior, but one that appeared to be aging gracefully with a timeless quality. In reality, many of the stations remodeled in the 1960s have aged faster than those they replaced, and one is left to wonder if Francis could see this coming.

In the 1950s and '60s, assignments seem evenly divided between "razing of" and "progress on" photos. It was a time of incredible change for the CTA, as the new agency was fighting to maintain its dwindling ridership against the lure of the automobile and new superhighways. The CTA abandoned six of its old elevated lines and replaced them with new lines along the Eisenhower, Kennedy and Dan Ryan expressways. It renovated the old stations and purchased modern equipment, dubbed "New Look" trains and buses. This was a bittersweet time for those who loved the old look, and many Chicagoans carefully followed each passing with the reverence reserved for loved ones.

THE FIRST OF 570 GREEN HORNET-STYLE STREETCARS IS LOADED ON A FLATBED TRAIN IN FRONT OF A CTA PHOTOGRAPHER IN 1953. THE STREETCAR WAS SHIPPED TO ST. LOUIS TO BE STRIPPED FOR PARTS THAT WERE USED TO BUILD THE 6000-SERIES RAPID TRANSIT CARS.

A large portion of the photo work has been scattered and lost—sent to the claims, legal or personnel departments decades ago and discarded over the years for legal and logistical reasons. Accident photographs show up in flea markets and online sales periodically. Some CTA employees managed to salvage photographs earmarked for destruction. What remains, generally, is what was classified as public service work. It forms the heart of the collection—photographs that show how the transit system and the city developed.

The archive has moved from building to building and department to department as the CTA reorganized. Today, it remains locked in drawers at the CTA's headquarters at 567 West Lake Street just west of the Loop. The 20,000 prints are filed alphabetically: Advertising, Airports, Alarms, etc. The collection of 200,000 negatives starts on March 11, 1949, with photographs of the Western Avenue and 79th Street Terminal, and continues through a retirement dinner on November 18, 1994, the year the photo department was disbanded. Since then, departments are responsible for their own photography.

This story begins around 1875 and tells a century-long narrative. Chicago begins to look familiar starting in the mid-1970s—we will leave that chapter to future generations.

⁜   ⁜   ⁜   ⁜   ⁜

The photographs in this book are decades old, but this is not a book of nostalgia. In fact, much of what you see on these pages is still here.

Many of the stations are the same. They may lie under layers of paint, hide behind or alongside new machinery, but you can still see the original bricks and wood if you pause to look. Even many old streetcar tracks and granite pavers still exist—though buried under inches of asphalt. Next time you see a street torn open, take a peek into the hole. You might see streetcar track, and even smell pneumatic oil.

Of course, the rapid transit's high line, 20 feet above the city, and subway, 40 feet below, are very much like the tracks that were originally built. The trains are sleeker and more powerful today, but they don't generally operate much faster than the first ones.

To see it all, though, you need to look. And we rarely stop to do that. We think about the next train as we hurry on our way. And at night, when the pace slows, we are preoccupied by our thoughts of the day or eager to get home. So the stations and their stories go unnoticed.

This archive shows a transit system of dignity and democracy. The system belongs to us all. Yes, it maddens us. It makes us late. But it connects us to an unending parade of humanity. This is where many of us experience the real city—from business deals to confidence games. This is where we try to avoid eye contact. But this is also where we meet—if ever so briefly.

"We both got on the packed train at Washington/Wells yesterday at 5:15/5:30ish," reads a Craigslist Missed Connection ad. "Somehow we ended up sitting across from each other and reading the same book (great taste by the way!). Toward Fullerton the crazy el conductor made a remark that made us both smile and look at each other. I really wish I would have said something to you then! And have been thinking about it since."

This network of machines was designed just to get us from one place to another. Yet it inspires and stimulates us. Lost in imagination, we stare out the window of a bus or "L," looking into Loop offices and neighborhood apartment buildings, barely aware of the transit web that links us. These photos tell that story—Chicago's story—of a city of travelers.

OFFICIALS WATCH AS A TRAIN HEADS INTO THE SUBWAY TUNNEL NEAR DIVISION STREET AFTER LEAVING THE DAMEN AVENUE STATION. PHOTOGRAPHERS CROWDED INTO THE LEAD CAR OF THE MILWAUKEE-DEARBORN SUBWAY'S INAUGURAL RUN.

❊ PRAIRIE TRACKS ❊

The first spike for Chicago's first streetcar line was driven into the earth at State and Randolph streets in 1859. By April, one track was built down State to the Southern Hotel on 12th Street. Cars pulled by horses along a track were an immediate success. The State Street line was soon extended to the city limits at 34th Street and later across the prairie to 39th Street.

"It is conceded that there is cause for complaint consequent upon the crowded condition of the cars on State Street," wrote railroad owner Frank Parmelee in nineteenth-century formality.

"But your notice thereof will lead the public to believe that no effort is being made by the company to minister to the comfort and convenience of the public in this respect.

"The contrary is the fact."

Horse cars eventually gave way to cable cars on the busiest routes, and finally both horse and cable gave way to electric streetcars. Success brought crowding, and crowding brought complaints. Public transportation was born in the city on the move. ☩

HORSE-DRAWN STREETCARS HEAD DOWN STATE STREET AT 3-MILES-PER-HOUR. THE PHOTO WAS TAKEN BEFORE TROUGHS WERE DUG IN THE CENTER OF THE STREETCAR TRACKS TO ACCOMMODATE CABLE CARS. THIS VIEW LOOKS NORTH AT MADISON STREET. HORSE CARS KEPT WORKING IN CHICAGO UNTIL 1906.

FAR LEFT: A HORSE CAR TRAVELS
DOWN ADAMS STREET NEAR THE
U.S. POST OFFICE AND CUSTOM
HOUSE AS IT APPROACHES CLARK
STREET (AT BOTTOM EDGE OF
PHOTO). LEFT: CABLE CARS BEGAN
REPLACING HORSE CARS IN 1882.
HERE AN INBOUND TWO-CAR
CABLE TRAIN HEADS OUT OF THE
LASALLE STREET TUNNEL UNDER
THE CHICAGO RIVER AS AN OUT-
BOUND CAR TAKES THE CURVE AT
LASALLE AND RANDOLPH STREETS.
CHICAGO HAD THE LARGEST FLEET
OF CABLE CARS IN THE NATION
DURING THE 1880S.

THE FIRST IMPRESSION WHICH A STRANGER RECEIVES ON ARRIVING IN CHICAGO IS THAT OF THE DIRT, THE DANGER AND THE INCONVENIENCE OF THE STREETS. THOSE ACCUSTOMED TO THE CARE THAT IS TAKEN IN CIVILIZED CITIES TO KEEP THE ROADWAY LEVEL AND SAFE FOR TEAMS AND CARRIAGES STAND SIMPLY AGHAST AT THE WAY IN WHICH THE THOROUGHFARES ARE CORDUROYED BY ILL-LAID, OLD-FASHIONED STREET CAR LINES, THE FLANGE OF WHICH PROJECTS SO MUCH ABOVE THE BODY OF THE RAIL ON WHICH THE TRAFFIC RUNS AS TO BE PERPETUALLY WRENCHING WHEELS OFF THE AXLE. THE CIVILIZED MAN MARVELS AND KEEPS ON HIS WAY.

IF CHRIST CAME TO CHICAGO! BY WILLIAM T. STEAD

HORSE CARS COMPETE WITH CARRIAGES AND WAGONS AT HAYMARKET SQUARE ON RANDOLPH STREET JUST WEST OF DESPLAINES STREET IN 1890. THE STATUE HONORING EIGHT POLICEMEN KILLED IN THE 1886 HAYMARKET RIOT WAS INSTALLED THE PREVIOUS YEAR.

I'VE NOTICED LATELY THAT MY SENSE OF TIME PASSING IS DIFFERENT; IT SEEMS TO RUN SLOWER THAN OTHER PEOPLE'S. AN AFTERNOON CAN BE LIKE A DAY TO ME; AN EL RIDE CAN BE AN EPIC JOURNEY.

THE TIME TRAVELER'S WIFE BY AUDREY NIFFENEGGER

CHICAGO'S FIRST ELECTRICALLY POWERED ELEVATED RAILROAD STREAKS THROUGH THE WORLD'S COLUMBIAN EXPOSITION IN 1893. THE THREE-MILE-LONG COLUMBIAN INTRAMURAL RAILWAY WAS BUILT TO SHOW HOW AN ELECTRIFIED THIRD-RAIL COULD POWER A TRAIN. THE TRACK WAS TORN DOWN AFTER THE FAIR CLOSED. CHICAGO'S FIRST PERMANENT ELEVATED LINE, THE SOUTH SIDE "L," WAS BUILT TO CONNECT DOWNTOWN AND THE FAIR SITE IN JACKSON PARK. THIS LINE, OPENED IN 1892, WAS POWERED BY STEAM LOCOMOTIVES DURING ITS FIRST SIX YEARS.

CHICAGO'S SECOND PERMANENT ELEVATED RAILROAD, THE LAKE STREET "L," OPENED IN 1893, EXTENDING WEST FROM DOWNTOWN TO CALIFORNIA AVENUE, AND LATER TO THE SUBURB OF OAK PARK. THE CITY'S FIRST RAPID TRANSIT CARS, BUILT FROM 1892 TO 1909, WERE MADE PRIMARILY OF WOOD. LEFT: A DERRICK HELPS CONSTRUCT THE LINE AT ROCKWELL STREET IN 1892. ABOVE: THE "L" IS POWERED BY A STEAM ENGINE AT OAKLEY AVENUE. STEAM WAS REPLACED ON THE LINE BY ELECTRICALLY SELF-PROPELLED CARS IN 1896.

LEFT: AT FIRST, THE LAKE STREET "L" ENDED ITS JOURNEY DOWNTOWN ON ELEVATED TRACKS ABOVE MARKET STREET (NOW WACKER DRIVE) AT MADISON STREET—SEVERAL BLOCKS WEST OF THE HEART OF DOWNTOWN. IN 1897, THE LINE WAS EXTENDED EAST ALONG LAKE STREET TO WABASH AVENUE. ABOVE: INVENTOR FRANK SPRAGUE (WATCHING MOTORMAN) DIRECTS A TEST OF THE SOUTH SIDE "L" ON THE HARRISON STREET CURVE JUST SOUTH OF THE LOOP IN 1898. SPRAGUE, LATER KNOWN AS THE FATHER OF ELECTRIC TRACTION (AS PUBLIC TRANSIT WAS THEN CALLED), PRODUCED A REVOLUTIONARY DEVICE THAT ALLOWED A SINGLE MOTORMAN TO RUN SEVERAL MOTORIZED RAPID TRANSIT CARS IN UNISON.

PANORAMIC VIEW LOOKING NORTHEAST FROM THE INTERSECTION OF FRANKLIN AND HUBBARD STREETS IN 1900. THE TRACK, BUILT BY THE NORTHWESTERN ELEVATED RAILROAD COMPANY, CONNECTED DOWNTOWN TO WILSON AVENUE ON THE NORTH SIDE. SINCE SERVICE BEGAN ON MAY 31, 1900, THIS CURVE HAS BEEN REALIGNED AND EASED TWICE. THE COMPANY OPENED A BRANCH TO THE RAVENSWOOD NEIGHBORHOOD IN 1907, AND LATER EXTENDED ITS MAIN LINE TO LINDEN AVENUE IN THE NORTHERN SUBURB OF WILMETTE.

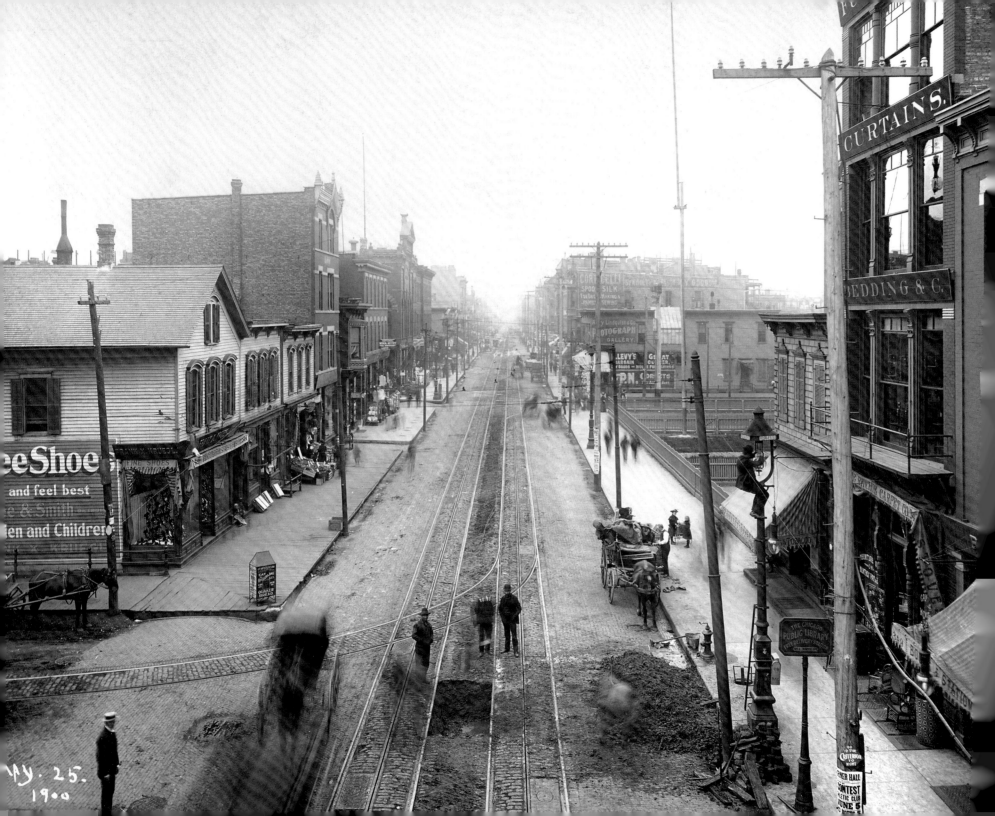

ABOVE: A SOUTHBOUND NORTHWESTERN "L" PULLS INTO THE CHICAGO AVENUE STATION ON THE THIRD DAY OF SERVICE, JUNE 2, 1900. THE STATION, AT 300 WEST CHICAGO, WAS NOT YET COMPLETE. LEFT: A LAMPLIGHTER CLIMBS A DIVISION STREET LIGHT POLE AT ORLEANS STREET IN THIS VIEW LOOKING WEST FROM THE NORTHWESTERN ELEVATED TRACKS IN 1900. A SHORT STRETCH OF DIVISION WAS SERVED BY CABLE CARS.

PAST GREY WOODEN PORCHES AND SECOND FLOOR CLOTHESLINES, BLACK IRON FIRE ESCAPES, BACKYARDS OF MORNING GLORIES, WHITE CURTAINS FLYING THROUGH OPEN KITCHEN WINDOWS, MEN IN THEIR UNDERSHIRTS DRINKING BEER ON STOOPS, CHILDREN PLAYING IN ALLEYS, THE SMOKE AND GRITTY SMELL OF FACTORIES, ROWS OF WOMEN AT SEWING MACHINES, HUGE OPEN BARRELS OF PICKLES, OTHER NEIGHBORHOODS. . . . THE EL WAS THE STREETCAR IN ASCENSION, THE DREAM OF FLIGHT MADE REAL, OUR FIRST VIEW OF A FALLING-AWAY SMALL WORLD THROUGH THE EYES OF A BIRD, THE COCKPIT OF A FLYING TIGER, THE VISION OF AN ANGEL. A CELESTIAL CONNECTION.

THEN BACK TO EARTH AGAIN.

ADAPTED FROM **NEIGHBORHOOD** BY NORBERT BLEI

THE BEND OF THE NORTHWESTERN LINE LOOKING EAST FROM HALSTED STREET JUST SOUTH OF NORTH AVENUE IN 1900. THE NORTHWESTERN HAD A FOUR-TRACK MAIN LINE, WHICH MADE IT POSSIBLE FOR THE COMPANY TO RUN LOCAL AND EXPRESS TRAINS FROM WILSON AVENUE TO CHICAGO AVENUE. THE FOUR TRACKS MERGED INTO JUST TWO AS THEY APPROACHED THE CENTRAL BUSINESS DISTRICT.

23

JAN. 25 1900

Feb. 2. 96.

34

FAR LEFT: CONSTRUCTION OF THE
NORTHWESTERN "L" STRUCTURE
LOOKING SOUTH FROM FUL-
LERTON AVENUE IN 1896. LEFT:
FOOTINGS ARE INSTALLED ON
THE LINE AT MONTANA STREET
IN 1896 AS IT HEADS NORTH.
CONSTRUCTION OF THE ELEVAT-
ED, WHICH WAS PROMOTED BY
TYCOON CHARLES YERKES, WAS
DELAYED FOR SEVERAL YEARS
DURING THE 1890S DUE TO FI-
NANCIAL PROBLEMS.

THE ELECTRIC STREETCAR, WITH ITS TROLLEY POLE REACHING FOR THE OVERHEAD ELECTRIFIED WIRE, FIRST APPEARED ON CHICAGO STREETS IN 1893. ABOVE: THE OPEN STREETCAR, LIKE THIS ONE THAT SERVED THE FAR SOUTH SIDE, WAS A JOY OF SUMMER AT THE TURN OF THE CENTURY. RIGHT: EVEN GEARED FOR WINTER, EARLY STREETCARS WERE BITTERLY COLD BECAUSE THEY WERE NOT EQUIPPED WITH HEATERS. THIS CAR, PROBABLY AT LINCOLN PARK, WAS PHOTOGRAPHED IN 1897.

His eyes were wild and his hair flying, and he was breathing hoarsely, like a wounded bull; but the people on the (street) car did not notice this particularly—perhaps it seemed natural to them that a man who smelled as Jurgis smelled should exhibit an aspect to correspond. They began to give way before him as usual. The conductor took his nickel gingerly, with the tips of his fingers, and then left him with the platform to himself.

The Jungle by Upton Sinclair

A trolley car crosses the Madison Street Bridge heading west in a sea of bridge traffic. The Market Street "L" track, with a Lake Street train, is in the background.

WITHOUT THINKING ABOUT IT, DAY BECAME A CREATURE OF THE CITY. WHAT SHE LOVED WAS ALL OF IT: THE STREETCARS SHE TOOK TO AND FROM WORK EVERY DAY OF THE WEEK, FIRST TRAVELING NORTH ON COTTAGE GROVE AVENUE AND THEN, WHEN THE CONDUCTOR CALLED OUT 22ND STREET, STEPPING OFF WITH THE CROWD AND TRANSFERRING WEST TO ASHLAND AVENUE. MOSTLY SHE WAS ABLE TO GET A SEAT BY THE WINDOW ON THE SECOND STREETCAR, SO SHE COULD WATCH THE SMOKE-STACKS BELCHING DARK GREY INTO THE SKY AND THE PEOPLE RUSHING ACROSS BUSY STREETS, EVERYBODY WITH SOMEWHERE THEY HAD TO BE. . . . SHE LOVED LIFE IN THE NORTH, AND SHE LOVED CHICAGO.

ANOTHER WAY HOME: THE TANGLED ROOTS OF RACE IN ONE CHICAGO FAMILY
BY RONNE HARTFIELD

A CABLE CAR TOWS A TRAILER AND AN ELECTRIC STREETCAR EASTBOUND PAST THE NEW CAR-SON PIRIE & SCOTT DEPARTMENT STORE AT STATE AND MADISON STREETS IN 1904. ELECTRIC OP-ERATION OF STREETCARS IN THE LOOP WAS PROHIBITED UNTIL 1906 BECAUSE OF CONCERNS ABOUT TROLLEY WIRES CLUT-TERING THE THOROUGHFARES. FOLLOWING PAGES: THE CHANG-ING CITY LANDSCAPE—MADISON STREET AND KEDZIE AVENUE IN 1910 (LEFT) AND IN 1912 (RIGHT).

FAR LEFT: TRAIN EMPLOYEES POSE ON THE STEPS OF THE NORTH WATER STREET TERMINAL AROUND 1920. THE TWO-BLOCK STUB TERMINAL WAS USED FOR EVENING RUSH-HOUR ELEVATED TRAINS AND OCCASIONALLY FOR NORTH SHORE INTERURBAN TRAINS. THE ENTRANCE WAS AT CLARK STREET AND CARROLL AVENUE, JUST EAST OF THE PRESENT SITE OF THE MERCHANDISE MART. LEFT: PASSENGERS TEST THE FANCY UPHOLSTERY OF THE 4000-SERIES STEEL RAPID TRANSIT CARS THAT WERE KNOWN AS PLUSHIES. THEY WERE EQUIPPED WITH FANS AND GLASS LAMPSHADES.

ABOVE: METROPOLITAN WEST SIDE ELEVATED RAILROAD'S MAIN LINE LOOKING WEST TOWARD THE CANAL STREET STATION IN 1924. THE MET WAS THE WORLD'S FIRST PERMANENT ELECTRIC RAPID TRANSIT LINE WHEN IT OPENED IN 1895. IT OPERATED FOUR ROUTES: LOGAN SQUARE, HUMBOLDT PARK, GARFIELD PARK AND DOUGLAS PARK. RIGHT: A FLAG-RAISING CEREMONY TO CELEBRATE THE END OF WORLD WAR I AT THE LOGAN SQUARE STATION, NEAR KEDZIE AVENUE AND LOGAN BOULEVARD.

ABOVE: TOWER 18 AT "THE BUSIEST RAILROAD JUNCTION IN THE WORLD," OVER LAKE AND WELLS STREETS. TOWERMEN HANDLED MORE THAN 1,000 TRAINS A DAY TRAVELLING TO OR FROM THE UNION LOOP, A HUGE RECTANGULAR TURNAROUND THAT STILL SURROUNDS THIRTY-FIVE BLOCKS OF THE CENTRAL BUSINESS DISTRICT. ALL FOUR ORIGINAL ELEVATED LINES USED THE UNION LOOP. LEFT: ANOTHER FLAG DAY CELEBRATION, THIS ONE AT THE 56TH AVENUE YARD IN CICERO ON THE DOUGLAS PARK LINE, IN 1918.

⊰ Men & Machines ⊱

The technological achievements that brought electric streetcars and elevated trains to Chicago were opposed at first. Residents considered overhead trolley lines, which formed a web above the street, unsightly. They worried that trains would fall from the high line.

But all that changed on May 27, 1892, when Engine No. 15 hauled six olive-green and yellow coaches on the first trip down the Alley "L" from Congress Street to 39th Street in nine-and-a-half minutes.

Housewives and domestics waved handkerchiefs, towels and aprons at the passing train, and mechanics waved their tools, the *Chicago Tribune* reported. "The people along the line were not surprised when the train rushed by, but to say that the dogs, cats, and horses were is stating a fact mildly.

"One big Newfoundland, who was basking in the sunshine on 12th Street, looked up with a startled expression as the cars whizzed by overhead, put its tail between its legs, and scuttled away just as rapidly as its power of locomotion would permit, ever and anon looking back to see if 'the thing' was chasing it."

For the first time, the words "rapid transit" took on new meaning. ⊱

MORE THAN 300 MEN WORKED AT THE LARRABEE CAR BARN IN 1900. THE BARN, ONE OF THE CITY'S LARGEST AT THE TIME, HOUSED HORSE-DRAWN STREET-CARS, CABLE CARS AND ELECTRIC STREETCARS AT 2011-41 NORTH LARRABEE STREET. (PHOTO BY O.C. HUDDLESTON.)

RIGHT: A TURBINE IN THE MET-
ROPOLITAN WEST SIDE ELEVATED
POWERHOUSE. EARLY TRANSIT
COMPANIES GENERATED THEIR
OWN ELECTRICITY, USING COAL
TO HEAT WATER AND PRODUCE
STEAM, WHICH SPUN TURBINES
THAT PRODUCED ELECTRIC-
ITY. THE HUGE POWERHOUSE,
NEAR THROOP AND VAN BUREN
STREETS, WAS TORN DOWN IN
THE 1950S TO MAKE WAY FOR
THE CONGRESS (NOW EISENHOW-
ER) EXPRESSWAY. FAR RIGHT: THE
HOWARD TOWER, ADJACENT TO
THE HOWARD YARD AND STATION
IN ROGERS PARK, WAS EQUIPPED
WITH AN AUTOMATED ELECTRO-
PNEUMATIC INTERLOCKING SYS-
TEM THAT HELPED PREVENT AC-
CIDENTS. THE YARD WAS BUILT
IN 1919; THE MODERN EQUIP-
MENT WAS ADDED FOUR YEARS
LATER.

ABOVE: INSIDE A MATCHBOX ELECTRIC STREETCAR, WHICH HELD ONLY 36 PASSENGERS. THESE ROUGH-RIDING, NOISY STREETCARS CARRIED ON FOR ABOUT A HALF-CENTURY STARTING IN 1903. LEFT: TWO-CAR STREETCAR "TRAINS" WERE TRIED ON A FEW BUSY LINES DURING THE 1920S WITH LITTLE SUCCESS. THIS STREETCAR TRAILER WAS BUILT IN 1921.

RIGHT: SOME OF THE FIRST STEEL
RAPID TRANSIT CARS, NICKNAMED
"BALDIES" DUE TO THEIR SMOOTH
ROOF LINES, HAD SEATS ALIGNED
AGAINST THE WALL, CREATING THE
LOOK OF A BOWLING ALLEY. STEEL
CARS, MADE PRIMARILY WITH
METAL BODIES, DEBUTED IN 1915.
FAR RIGHT: A BALDIE IS SPRAY
PAINTED IN 1929 AT THE NILES
CENTER (NOW SKOKIE) SHOPS.
THE NORTHWESTERN ELEVATED
RAILROAD EXTENDED SERVICE TO
THE NORTHERN SUBURB IN 1925,
A YEAR AFTER TAKING OVER THE
NORTHWESTERN ELEVATED. THE
SHOPS, BUILT TWO YEARS LATER AT
OAKTON STREET AND HAMLIN AV-
ENUE, STILL OPERATE.

WHO IS BIGGER THAN THE CITY, OR THE CITY'S STREETS, OR THE CITY'S WILL? WHO IS STRONGER THAN THIS TWISTED SKY OF TROLLEY WIRES AND THIS ROOF OF SMOKE? WHO IS TALLER THAN THESE CHIMNEYS BELCHING SOOT OR THESE WATERTOWERS? AND WHO CAN BREATHE AGAINST THE SKY WITH THESE SMOKESTACKS?

KNOCK ON ANY DOOR BY WILLARD MOTLEY

BOXY TROLLEY BUSES PACK THE CHICAGO SURFACE LINES' NORTH AVENUE CARHOUSE, NEAR NORTH AND CICERO AVENUES. THE BUSES, WHICH LIKE STREETCARS WERE POWERED FROM OVER-HEAD WIRES, BEGAN OPERATING IN 1930. THE CITY'S FIRST GAS-POWERED BUSES WERE RUN BY THE CHICAGO MOTOR COACH COMPANY.

LEFT: RECEIVER'S WINDOW AT THE LIMITS CARBARN, 2684 NORTH CLARK STREET, IN 1930. THIS WAS WHERE TRAINMEN TURNED IN THEIR RECEIPTS, TRANSFERS AND PAPERWORK, AND PICKED UP TAGS THAT IDENTIFIED THEIR STREETCAR RUNS. THE WINDOW WAS MADE OF BULLET-RESISTANT GLASS AND INCLUDED GUN PORTS. FAR LEFT: WEST SHOPS, NEAR LAKE STREET AND HARDING AVENUE IN WEST GARFIELD PARK, WHERE STREETCAR WHEELS WERE MACHINED, ELECTRIC MOTORS OVERHAULED AND FRAMES WERE STRAIGHTENED. THE SHOPS HAD ENOUGH ROOM FOR 176 STREETCARS.

HIGH-VOLTAGE ALTERNATING CURRENT
HAD TO BE CONVERTED TO DIRECT CUR-
RENT IN ORDER TO RUN STREETCARS
AND RAPID TRANSIT TRAINS. RIGHT:
MEN OVERHAUL A ROTARY CONVERTER
AT THE DEARBORN SUBSTATION. FAR
RIGHT: CHIEF OPERATOR BILL DORGAN
THROWS BREAKERS THAT CONNECT
POWER TO THE TRACKS AT THE ILLINOIS
SUBSTATION OF THE CHICAGO SURFACE
LINES. BY THE 1930S, THE COMPANY
USED MORE POWER THAN DID ALL THE
HOMEOWNERS IN THE CITY.

UPKEEP OF THE STREETCAR LINES WAS CONSTANT. ABOVE: A CREW REMOVES A WELL-WORN 90-DEGREE TRACK-CROSSING AT STATE AND WASHINGTON STREETS IN 1923. RIGHT: PAVING BLOCK IS REMOVED OVER TIES SO WORKERS CAN REPAIR TRACK. STREETCAR COMPANIES WERE RESPONSIBLE FOR THE MAINTENANCE OF TRACK AREAS, AND HAD TO PLOW STREETCAR LINES IN WINTER.

BECAUSE MOTORMAN, CONDUCTORS AND DRIVERS OFTEN HAD HOURS TO KILL BETWEEN RUSH-HOUR SHIFTS, THE TRAINMEN'S ROOM BECAME A MAJOR PART OF THEIR DAY. ABOVE: THE 69TH STREET CARBARN, AT ASHLAND AVENUE. LEFT: THE ARCHER AVENUE CARBARN, AT ROCKWELL AVENUE, HAD A STAGE FOR LECTURES AND ENTERTAINMENT. A FEW OLD BARNS, INCLUDING THE ARCHER CARBARN, STILL EXIST, BUT ALL HAVE BEEN MODERNIZED.

ABOVE: A SUPERVISOR MONITORS THE POWER AT SUBSTATIONS IN THE CHICAGO RAPID TRANSIT COMPANY'S HEADQUARTERS, 72 WEST ADAMS STREET. SAMUEL INSULL COMBINED ALL FOUR "L" LINES TO FORM THE COMPANY IN 1924. LEFT: ANNUAL OPERATING AND ACCIDENT PREVENTION MEETING HELD FOR STREETCAR TRAINMEN BASED AT THE DIVSION CARBARN IN 1943. THE DIVISION CARBARN WAS REPLACED BY ROBERTO CLEMENTE HIGH SCHOOL AT WESTERN AVENUE.

❊ DESTINATIONS ❊

Because the Chicago Surface Lines, Chicago Rapid Transit Company and Chicago Motor Coach Company were rivals, all three firms mounted aggressive advertising campaigns to woo riders.

The Surface Lines emphasized its blanket coverage ("Serving All Chicago"), and branded itself as a "A 5-cent Fare to Everywhere." The Rapid Transit Company stressed speed ("Extra Time to Spend as You Wish"), and countered with "The Easy, Quick Way to Get About Chicago." And the Chicago Motor Coach Company pushed its upper-deck views ("Open Air to Everywhere"), and declared itself "The Boulevard Route."

While the majority of the companies' ads were line drawings, all three firms collected hundreds of city photos for in-house and advertising promotion campaigns. A few of the pictures were taken by the transit companies; most were purchased from major Chicago studios. The photos, still in the files at the Chicago Transit Authority, give a sense of what the city's major attractions were during the early decades of the twentieth century. Some still are; some are long forgotten. ❖

THE OPENING OF THE PALMOLIVE BUILDING, AT MICHIGAN AVENUE AND WALTON PLACE, IN 1929 EXTENDED THE CITY'S MAIN COMMERCIAL DISTRICT NORTH OF THE LOOP. A CHICAGO SURFACE LINES BROCHURE WROTE OF THE LINDBERGH SEARCHLIGHT: "THIS AERIAL BEACON IS CONSIDERED THE MOST POWERFUL EVER MADE."

RIGHT: THE ITALIAN COURT, 615 NORTH MICHIGAN AVENUE, BECAME MORE ACCESSIBLE IN THE 1920S AFTER THE MICHIGAN AVENUE BRIDGE OPENED. THE COURT—WITH GIFT SHOPS, GALLERIES, SALONS AND STUDIOS— ANTICIPATED THE DEVELOPMENT OF WHAT WAS CALLED "THE WORLD'S GREATEST THOROUGHFARE." FAR RIGHT: THE ROCKEFELLER CHAPEL, AT 5850 SOUTH WOODLAWN AVENUE. "TAKE SOUTH SIDE RAPID TRANSIT TRAINS MARKED 'JACKSON PARK' TO UNIVERSITY AVE. STATION," THE RAPID TRANSIT COMPANY ADVISED. "WALK NORTH ACROSS THE MIDWAY."

LEFT: BECAUSE THE WHITE CITY AMUSEMENT PARK WAS ON THE JACKSON PARK BRANCH "L" LINE, IT ATTRACTED CUSTOMERS FROM ALL OVER THE CITY. THIS PHOTO WAS TAKEN FROM THE ELEVATED PLATFORM AT 63RD STREET NEAR SOUTH PARKWAY (NOW MARTIN LUTHER KING DRIVE). ABOVE: THE CENTRAL AVENUE TROLLEY BUS LINE WAS THE SURFACE LINES' LONGEST "TRACKLESS TROLLEY" IN THE 1930S.

IN THE DISTANCE A YELLOW LIGHT SWINGS LIKE AN IDLE LANTERN OVER THE CAR TRACKS. SO THE NEWSPAPER MAN STOPS AT THE CORNER AND WAITS. THIS IS THE OWL CAR. IT MAY NOT STOP. SOMETIMES CARS HAVE A HABIT OF ROARING BY WITH AN INSULTING INDIFFERENCE TO THE PEOPLE WAITING FOR THEM TO STOP AT THE CORNER. AT SUCH MOMENTS ONE FEELS A FINE RAGE, AS IF LIFE ITSELF HAD INSULTED ONE. THERE HAVE BEEN INSTANCES OF MEN THROWING BRICKS THROUGH THE WINDOWS OF CARS THAT WOULDN'T STOP AND CHEERFULLY GOING TO JAIL FOR THE CRIME.

1001 AFTERNOONS IN CHICAGO BY BEN HECHT

A STREETCAR STREAKS PAST THE MCJUNKIN BUILDING, AT THE SOUTHWEST CORNER OF WILSON AVENUE AND BROADWAY. THE BUILDING, WHICH OPENED IN 1923, INCLUDED AN ENTRANCE TO THE WILSON AVENUE STATION IN UPTOWN.

ABOVE: BENEATH THE ELEVATED LINE ALONG VAN BUREN STREET IN 1928. LEFT: ONE YEAR AFTER THE FIRST SECTION OF WACKER DRIVE WAS COMPLETED, PLANS WERE ANNOUNCED FOR THE CONSTRUCTION OF THE MERCHANDISE MART NORTH OF THE CHICAGO RIVER. AT THE TIME, UPPER AND LOWER WACKER WAS ONLY AN EAST-WEST STREET CONNECTING MICHIGAN AVENUE WITH LAKE STREET. THE NORTH-SOUTH EXTENSION WAS COMPLETED DURING THE MID-1950S.

CHICAGO'S CANYONS. RIGHT: THE CHICAGO BOARD OF TRADE BUILDING BEFORE BEING CROWNED WITH ITS CERES STATUE. THE 45-STORY BUILDING AT 141 WEST JACKSON BOULEVARD OPENED IN 1930. FAR RIGHT: LOOKING WEST DOWN THE CHICAGO RIVER AT MICHIGAN AVENUE. "STEAMERS LEAVE FOR NEARBY MICHIGAN AND WISCONSIN RESORTS," A SURFACE LINES GUIDE WROTE ABOUT THE MICHIGAN AVENUE BRIDGE DOCK.

☀ Limits ☀

Chicagoans understood early the impact of efficient public transportation. Good streetcar or elevated service meant new homes and new neighborhoods. In 1888, a Lakeview resident wrote the *Chicago Tribune* that the South Side's Chicago City Railway Company was changing the face of Chicago.

"One great result of this is that property is rapidly advancing all along its line; indeed, throughout the whole South Side and its outlying towns," the man wrote. "The drift of population is certainly southward. Confidence is felt by property-owners beyond the immediate conveniences of the present extensions. Building for the last few years in that direction has been prodigious. Swampy lands have been reclaimed, subdivided, improved and palatial residences erected. There is no question whatever but that these superior facilities of transportation are the prime factors of the advancement of South Side suburban property over that of the North Side."

That population drift was soon to change. ☩

THE EDGE OF THE CITY. TRANSIT TRACKS OFTEN ANNOUNCED THE DIRECTION OF DEVELOPMENT. HERE A STREETCAR LINE EXTENDS PAST 79TH STREET AND CORNELL AVENUE IN 1915 IN THE SOUTH SHORE NEIGHBORHOOD. THE LINE RAN EAST-WEST DOWN 79TH FROM WESTERN AVENUE TO LAKE MICHIGAN.

THE METROPOLITAN'S GARFIELD PARK LINE WAS EXTENDED WEST FROM SUBURBAN FOREST PARK TO WESTCHESTER IN 1926, AND THEN SOUTH TO MANNHEIM ROAD AND 22ND STREET IN 1930. ABOVE: LOOKING NORTH FROM ROOSEVELT ROAD NEAR MANNHEIM IN 1926. RIGHT: THE TERMINAL AT 22ND IN 1930. DEVELOPERS ADVERTISED: "WHERE THE 'L' GOES, PROFIT GROWS," BUT THE DEPRESSION SLOWED GROWTH.

PHOTOGRAPHERS MADE A RE-
CORD OF THE WIDE-OPEN FARM-
LAND DURING CONSTRUCTION
OF THE SKOKIE VALLEY LINE,
WHICH CONNECTED THE HOW-
ARD STREET STATION AT THE
NORTHERN TIP OF CHICAGO TO
DEMPSTER STREET IN WHAT WAS
CALLED NILES CENTER. THESE
VIEWS WERE TAKEN OF OAK-
TON STREET IN 1924. "IT IS BE-
LIEVED THAT THE TERRITORY
TRIBUTARY TO THIS LINE WILL BE
RAPIDLY BUILT UP AND THAT IT
WILL SOON BECOME A VALUABLE
ADDITION TO THE COMPANY'S
SYSTEM," THE CHICAGO RAPID
TRANSIT COMPANY PREDICTED
IN ITS 1925 ANNUAL REPORT.

C. N. S. & N. R. R. Co.
OAKTON ST. VIEW SOUTH.
9-25-24.

STREET-CAR LINES HAD BEEN EXTENDED FAR OUT INTO THE OPEN COUNTRY IN ANTICIPATION OF RAPID GROWTH. THE CITY HAD LAID MILES AND MILES OF STREETS AND SEWERS THROUGH REGIONS WHERE, PERHAPS, ONE SOLITARY HOUSE STOOD OUT ALONE——A PIONEER OF THE POP- ULOUS WAYS TO BE. THERE WERE REGIONS OPEN TO THE SWEEPING WINDS AND RAIN, WHICH WERE YET LIGHTED THROUGHOUT THE NIGHT WITH LONG, BLINKING LINES OF GAS-LAMPS, FLUTTERING IN THE WIND. NARROW BOARD WALKS EXTENDED OUT, PASSING HERE A HOUSE, AND THERE A STORE, AT FAR INTERVALS, EVENTUALLY ENDING ON THE OPEN PRAIRIE.

SISTER CARRIE BY THEODORE DREISER

THAT SAME DAY, PHOTOGRAPHS WERE TAKEN ON NEARBY MAIN STREET LOOKING EAST FROM WHAT APPEARS TO BE PRESENT SKOKIE BOULEVARD. THE LINE WAS BUILT BY SAMUEL INSULL'S CHICAGO NORTH SHORE & MIL- WAUKEE RAILROAD AND SHARED WITH HIS CHICAGO RAPID TRAN- SIT COMPANY.

ABOVE: SCHREIBER ROAD (NOW KNOWN AS KOSTNER AVENUE IN SKOKIE) STATION ON THE SKOKIE VALLEY LINE IN 1924. RIGHT: PHOTOS SHOW HOW QUICKLY THE LINE'S ASBURY AVENUE STATION, AT BRUMMEL STREET IN EVANSTON, WAS CONSTRUCTED DURING EIGHT WEEKS IN 1925.

C.N.S. & N.R.R.Co.
VIEW WEST FROM DODGE AVE.
EVANSTON ILLS 7-17-24.

No 7.

ABOVE: A WORK TRAIN DELIVERS FILL NEAR DODGE AVENUE IN EVANSTON TO BUILD THE NORTH SHORE'S SKOKIE VALLEY LINE IN 1924.
RIGHT: CATENARY BRIDGES HOLD OVERHEAD WIRES THAT POWERED THE RAPID TRANSIT AND INTERURBAN TRAINS. THE VIEW LOOKS WEST
FROM THE EAST PRAIRIE-CRAWFORD STATION IN NILES CENTER, ONE MONTH AFTER THE RAPID TRANSIT LINE OPENED IN 1925. WHEN
CRAWFORD AVENUE WAS BUILT, IT CROSSED THE TRACKS AT THE END OF THE FENCE.

❊ MEET THE PUBLIC ❊

"Do you give the conductor a dollar bill when even change or a dime would speed things up?" asked a conductor's wife. "Do you fold your transfer into little sections and give it to the conductor to unfold? Do you hold last minute conversations on the steps of the car? . . . Do you try to pass a bad transfer when you know it's no good? (The men are no fools, you know.)"

Her questions, directed to rapid transit riders, underscored the tense relationship between riders and employees.

Running streetcars, trains and buses was never easy. Collecting money, issuing transfers, providing directions and enforcing rules took patience and skill that didn't always come naturally.

To that end, the Chicago Surface Lines staged and photographed typical situations to create a film in 1935 that was used to teach employees on the right and wrong ways to handle and defuse difficult passengers. Some images from the film were reproduced in the company's in-house publication, *Surface Service.* A few have survived. ❖

THE CHICAGO SURFACE LINES' "MEET THE PUBLIC" FILM OFFERED ADVICE TO TRAINMEN. "THE PASSENGER WHO BLOCKS THE ENTRANCES USUALLY DOES SO THOUGHTLESSLY," THE NARRATOR ADVISED. "A FRIENDLY REQUEST IS ALL THAT IS NEEDED TO GET HIM TO MOVE FORWARD."

"THE INEBRIATED PASSENGER IS ALWAYS A PROBLEM," THE FILM FOREWARNS. "TACT IS BETTER THAN FORCE."

RIGHT: "IT TAKES TWO TO MAKE AN ARGUMENT. THE CONDUCTOR GAINS NOTHING BY ARGUING WITH AN ANGRY PASSENGER."

❋ OLD REDS ❋

Starting in the 1920s, the Chicago Surface Lines undertook a project to document many major intersections within the city limits. Using large-format cameras, company photographers created dramatic views of city neighborhoods and the Loop.

Apparently taken to show how streetcars ran through the city, the pictures now show so much more. Cops on the beat, taut trolley wires, wide-open spaces, buildings lathered in terra cotta, vibrant nightlife, second-floor chop suey joints and grand movie palaces. They are snapshots of a city lost in time.

And they show the old reds, the ubiquitous streetcars that rattled through the streets getting louder and louder with each decade. These antiquated trolleys brought romance to the city. Just ask those who rode them.

"These old red streetcars were classed as obsolete," wrote Frank J. Kocka in 1952, "though they were cleaner, warmer and more practical than today's CTA streetcars." But only two years later, the old reds were gone. ✛

WACKER DRIVE AND CLARK STREET IN 1931. THIS STREETCAR, KNOWN AS A SEDAN, WAS ONE OF THE CHICAGO SURFACE LINES' MOST HANDSOME. PAINTED CARMINE RED AND CREAM, IT RAN PRIMARILY ON SEVERAL LONG NORTH-SOUTH ROUTES, INCLUDING THE CLARK-WENTWORTH LINE FROM 1929 TO 1953.

NIGHT AND DAY ON RANDOLPH STREET. ABOVE: LOOKING EAST FROM CLARK STREET IN 1931. LEFT: LOOKING WEST FROM STATE STREET IN 1933. "ALL LEADING THEATERS ARE REACHED CONVENIENTLY ON THE RAPID TRANSIT LINES."

ABOVE: "THE PARKS ARE NOW A WILDERNESS OF WOODLAND BEAUTY," ADVERTISED THE CHICAGO SURFACE LINES, "INVITING LONG DAYS OF ENJOYMENT OUT OF DOORS." HERE A MADISON STREETCAR AND TRAILER HEADS THROUGH GARFIELD PARK IN 1929. LEFT: THE OLD FEDERAL BUILDING IN 1932. THIS VIEW IS LOOKING EAST ON QUINCY STREET TOWARD CLARK STREET.

COME YOU, CARTOONISTS,
HANG ON A STRAP WITH ME HERE
AT SEVEN O'CLOCK IN THE MORNING
ON A HALSTED STREET CAR.

TAKE YOUR PENCILS
AND DRAW THESE FACES.
TRY WITH YOUR PENCILS FOR THESE CROOKED FACES,
THAT PIG-STICKER IN ONE CORNER—HIS MOUTH—
THAT OVERALL FACTORY GIRL—HER LOOSE CHEEKS.

FIND FOR YOUR PENCILS
A WAY TO MARK YOUR MEMORY
OF TIRED EMPTY FACES.

AFTER THEIR NIGHT'S SLEEP,
IN THE MOIST DAWN
AND COOL DAYBREAK,
FACES
TIRED OF WISHES,
EMPTY OF DREAMS.

HALSTED STREET CAR BY CARL SANDBURG

ONE OF THE BUSIEST INTERSECTIONS ON THE SOUTH SIDE WAS 63RD AND HALSTED STREETS IN ENGLEWOOD. THIS VIEW IS LOOKING EAST ON 63RD TOWARD HALSTED IN 1934. ENTERTAINER BOB HOPE FOUND HIS FIRST PROFESSIONAL SUCCESS ON THE VAUDEVILLE STAGE OF THE NEIGHBORHOOD'S STRATFORD THEATER IN THE LATE 1920S.

CHICAGO NEIGHBORHOODS WERE LIKE SMALL TOWNS, WITH MOST EVERYTHING RESIDENTS NEEDED WITHIN WALKING DISTANCE. SOME BUSINESS DISTRICTS WERE EERILY SIMILIAR. ABOVE: LOOKING WEST ALONG ROOSEVELT ROAD AT KEDZIE AVENUE. LEFT: LOOKING WEST ALONG NORTH AVENUE AT CRAWFORD AVENUE (NOW PULASKI ROAD) IN HUMBOLDT PARK. BOTH PHOTOS WERE TAKEN IN 1934.

ABOVE: JANE ADDAMS' HULL HOUSE SUCCEEDED AS ONE OF THE NATION'S FIRST SETTLEMENT HOUSES PARTLY BECAUSE IT WAS ON A STREETCAR LINE. THIS PHOTO WAS TAKEN NEAR HALSTED AND POLK STREETS IN 1935, THE YEAR OF ADDAMS' DEATH. RIGHT: LANE TECH, AT WESTERN AVENUE AND ADDISON STREET, WAS THE STATE'S LARGEST HIGH SCHOOL WHEN IT OPENED IN 1934 WITH A CLASS OF 9,000.

ABOVE: A STREETCAR HEADS PAST MUNICIPAL AIRPORT, CHICAGO'S FIRST, IN 1935. ONLY A SINGLE-TRACK SERVED THE AIRPORT. IT WAS RE-NAMED MIDWAY IN 1947. LEFT: LOOKING NORTH ON AVERS AVENUE TOWARD THE 26TH STREET STREETCAR LINE IN SOUTH LAWNDALE.

ABOVE: THE CHICAGO RAPID TRANSIT COMPANY ADVERTISED "THE GHETTO" AS ONE OF ITS POINTS OF INTEREST. THIS VIEW SHOWS MAXWELL STREET LOOKING EAST TOWARD HALSTED STREET. RIGHT: STREETCARS AND A CHICAGO MOTOR COACH BUS CONVERGE IN FRONT OF WRIGLEY FIELD BEFORE GAME 4 OF THE 1935 WORLD SERIES. THE DETROIT TIGERS BEAT THE CUBS THAT DAY AND WENT ON TO WIN THE SERIES 4 GAMES TO 2.

When I was a kid, the best days of the summer were spent at the beach.

The cinder-covered school yard was too hot and dusty for softball. The alleys were so choked with flies and garbage smells that hunting bottles for their two-cent deposits was no fun.

So we grabbed our itchy wool trunks and a fried-egg sandwich, rode a North Avenue streetcar to the end of the line, and there it was—the big, blue, cool, clean lake.

You could smell it and taste it long before you saw it.

Chicago Sun-Times column by Mike Royko

EASTBOUND CHICAGO AVENUE STREETCAR PASSES LAKE SHORE PARK ON ITS WAY TO NAVY PIER.

ABOVE: THE CHICAGO AVENUE STREETCAR TURNED SOUTHEAST ALONG LAKE SHORE DRIVE AND RAN TO NAVY PIER ON GRAND AVENUE UNTIL 1937. RIGHT: THE STONY ISLAND STREETCAR RAN FROM THE PIER ON A CIRCUITOUS ROUTE TO 93RD STREET. HERE IT HEADS DOWN STONY ISLAND SOUTH AT 77TH STREET IN 1934.

FIVE- AND SIX-CORNER INTERSECTIONS MADE FOR COMPLEX STREETCAR SWITCHING. ABOVE: LOOKING NORTHWEST UP MILWAUKEE AVENUE AS IT CROSSES HALSTED STREET AND GRAND AVENUE IN 1934. LEFT: DIVERSEY PARKWAY IN 1935 AS CLARK STREET HEADS NORTHWEST AND BROADWAY HEADS NORTHEAST. THE DIVERSEY THEATER IS NOW THE CENTURY SHOPPING CENTER.

ABOVE: TEMPORARY TRACKS MADE IT POSSIBLE FOR STREETCARS TO TRAVEL DIRECTLY TO THE CENTURY OF PROGRESS EXPOSITION IN 1933 AND 1934. HERE CARS TRAVEL UP SOUTH LAKE SHORE DRIVE IN A VIEW LOOKING NORTH FROM THE 23RD STREET ENTRANCE RAMP. LEFT: RADIO BROADCAST TOWERS DWARF SOUTH SIDE THEATERS AND NIGHTCLUBS LOOKING NORTH ON COTTAGE GROVE AVENUE FROM 63RD STREET IN 1934. THE TRIANON BALLROOM, AT 62ND STREET AND COTTAGE GROVE, IS IN THE BACKGROUND.

THE STREET CAR RUMBLED UP AND HE GOT ON AND RODE TO FORTY-SEVENTH STREET, WHERE HE TRANSFERRED TO AN EAST-BOUND CAR. HE LOOKED ANXIOUSLY AT THE DIM REFLECTION OF HIS BLACK FACE IN THE SWEATY WINDOWPANE. WOULD ANY OF THE WHITE FACES ALL ABOUT HIM THINK THAT HE HAD KILLED A RICH WHITE GIRL? NO! THEY MIGHT THINK HE WOULD STEAL A DIME, RAPE A WOMAN, GET DRUNK, OR CUT SOMEBODY; BUT TO KILL A MILLIONAIRE'S DAUGHTER AND BURN HER BODY? HE SMILED A LITTLE, FEELING A TINGLING SENSATION ENVELOPING ALL HIS BODY. HE SAW IT ALL VERY SHARPLY AND SIMPLY: ACT LIKE OTHER PEOPLE THOUGHT YOU OUGHT TO ACT, YET DO WHAT YOU WANTED.

NATIVE SON BY RICHARD WRIGHT

THE HEART OF BRONZEVILLE WAS 47TH STREET AND SOUTH PARKWAY AVENUE (NOW MARTIN LUTHER KING DRIVE). IN THIS VIEW, A 47TH STREET STREETCAR HEADS WEST PAST THE REGAL THEATER IN 1934. THE REGAL'S MAIN ENTRANCE WAS ON SOUTH PARKWAY JUST NORTH OF THE SAVOY BALLROOM.

CITY AND COUNTRY. ABOVE: A STREETCAR HEADS NORTH ALONG CRAWFORD AVENUE PAST WHAT IS NOW GOMPERS PARK NEAR FOSTER AVENUE IN 1924. LEFT: LOOKING NORTHWEST ON MILWAUKEE AVENUE AT ASHLAND AVENUE (DIVISION STREET IS BEHIND THE PHOTOGRAPHER). "EVERY THRIVING BUSINESS CENTER IN CHICAGO HAS GROWN UP AROUND A STREET CAR INTERSECTION," ADVERTISED THE SURFACE LINES.

ABOVE: CLARK STREET LOOKING EAST ALONG RIDGE AVENUE IN 1934. SENN HIGH SCHOOL AND THE NICOLAS KRANSZ HOUSE, BUILT IN 1848, ARE IN THE BACKGROUND. LEFT: LOOKING SOUTHEAST DOWN LINCOLN AVENUE AT THE INTERSECTION OF BELMONT AND ASHLAND AVENUES IN 1934. THE AUTOS ON THE RIGHT ARE HEADING UP ASHLAND. BELMONT IS BEHIND THE POLICE OFFICER.

129

THE DIFFERENT MODELS OF STREETCARS WERE KNOWN BY MANY NICKNAMES, INCLUDING TURTLEBACKS, MATCHBOXES, SEWING MACHINES, MUZZLE LOADERS, 169S, SUN PARLORS, OLD PULLMANS, BIG BRILLS, FLEXIBLE FLYERS, SEDANS, AND PETER WITTS. ABOVE: A NORTHBOUND 169 ON WABASH AVENUE AT ROOSEVELT ROAD IN 1944. RIGHT: ANOTHER 169 HEADS TOWARD CHICAGO'S BUSIEST INTERSECTION, STATE AND MADISON, THAT SAME YEAR.

RIGHT: MOTORMAN NICK ALVER SWINGS HIS CONTROLLER HANDLE AS HE GUIDES A STREETCAR INTO THE ELSTON CARBARN, AT ELSTON AVENUE AND ADDISON STREET, IN 1942. FAR RIGHT: MANY CARBARNS STARTED CLOSING AS THE OLD-STYLE STREETCARS WERE TAKEN OUT OF SERVICE. THIS ONE AT LINCOLN AND WRIGHTWOOD AVENUES WAS PHOTOGRAPHED IN ITS FINAL DAYS IN 1951.

⊰ STREAMLINERS ⊱

They were called the "Streetcars of Tomorrow." With leather seats and gears that hummed instead of whined, rubber padding and blinker doors that folded like origami, the streamlined, stainless-steel streetcars looked as if they came from a science fiction novel.

They were introduced because streetcars were starting to lose the battle of the street—to the automobile and to the bus.

"After several rides on this new vehicle I find they come up to everything a person could desire in the way of quiet, speedy, and comfortable transportation," wrote Chicagoan Emil Kurt a week after the new streetcars were introduced. "The name of this new vehicle could well be changed from that of the streetcar or trolley car to 'glide car.'"

Actually, the new vehicles were known as PCC cars, named for the Presidents' Conference Committee that designed them. In Chicago, they were known simply as "Blue Geese." ✝

THOUSANDS OF CHICAGOANS FILLED MADISON STREET FROM THE WESTERN CITY LIMITS AT AUSTIN BOULEVARD TO CANAL STREET DOWNTOWN TO SEE THE CITY'S NEW STREAMLINED STREETCARS AT A NIGHT TRANSIT PAGEANT ON NOVEMBER 12, 1936. HERE THEY SURROUND THE FIRST SIX DELIVERED STREETCARS AS THE CARS APPROACH KARLOV AVENUE.

RIGHT: MADISON STREET STREAM-
LINERS PASS EACH OTHER AT THE
WESTERN EDGE OF GARFIELD
PARK AT HAMLIN BOULEVARD.
FAR RIGHT: A BLUE GOOSE SNEAKS
PAST A LINE CREW THAT WAS RE-
PAIRING TROLLEY WIRE ABOVE
CLINTON STREET AT MADISON IN
1944.

RIGHT: THE VIEW FROM A BLUE
GOOSE IN 1936. "PROBABLY THE
MOST NOTICEABLE FEATURE OF
THE CAR IS ITS LACK OF NOISE,"
WROTE THE CHICAGO TRIBUNE.
FAR RIGHT: JUST AFTER THE WAR,
SIX BLUE GEESE CHANGED THEIR
STRIPES AS NEW COLOR SCHEMES
WERE APPLIED IN A TEST TO
DETERMINE HOW THE SECOND
GENERATION OF STREAMLINERS
WOULD BE PAINTED. HERE THEY
ARE LINED UP IN FRONT OF THE
KEDZIE CARBARN AT VAN BUREN
STREET.

✳ THE UNDERWORLD ⟿

Subways were built under Boston in 1897, under New York in 1904, and under Philadelphia in 1908. They didn't appear in Chicago until one minute after midnight on October 17, 1943, when the State Street subway debuted before thousands of Chicagoans who jammed the platforms from 16th Street on the South Side to Willow Street on the North Side.

"Almost everyone has had a ride in the new subway, but have they seen it as I have seen it?" asked Jeanne Fay later that year. She walked to the front of the first car, and described what she saw through the glass door.

"It was a thrilling sight: a great archway softly lighted at intervals extending before me for miles, carried me into fairyland. Here we were traveling at a great speed below the great City of Chicago, under the river and the Loop, in perfect comfort."

Breathless, she concluded: "How wonderful is the ingenuity of man!" ✝

LOOKING UP THE CONTRACTOR'S SHAFT THAT LED TO A SUBWAY CONSTRUCTION SITE. BUILDING BEGAN ON THE 3.8-MILE DEARBORN AND 4.9-MILE STATE SUBWAYS IN LATE 1938. THE SHAFT, AT STATE STREET NEAR CHICAGO AVENUE, WAS USED TO MOVE EQUIPMENT DOWN TO THE HORIZONTAL TRAIN TUBES 40 FEET UNDERGROUND.

LEFT: FOUR HUGE BORING MA-
CHINES WERE USED TO PUNCH
A TUNNEL 25 FEET IN DIAMETER
UNDER THE LOOP. PROPELLED BY
HYDRAULIC RETRACTABLE STEEL
JACKS, THE MACHINES WERE
KNOWN AS "BISCUIT CUTTERS"
BECAUSE THEY CUT THE CLAY IN
A SIMILAR MANNER. WITH THREE
CREWS WORKING AROUND THE
CLOCK, EACH CUTTER COULD
MOVE UP TO 25 FEET A DAY. IT
TOOK ONE YEAR TO PROGRESS
FROM 11TH AND STATE STREETS
NORTH TO WACKER DRIVE AND
STATE. FAR LEFT: AIR PRESSURE
WAS INCREASED IN THE EXCA-
VATION AREA TO HELP SUPPORT
THE ROOF AND WALLS. IN ORDER
TO ADJUST TO THE PRESSURE
CHANGE, WORKERS SAT IN AN
AIRLOCK, WHERE PRESSURE WAS
SLOWLY INCREASED.

RIGHT: A LEVEL OF WET BLUE CLAY, 30 TO 50 FEET DEEP UNDER THE LOOP, PRESENTED THE BIGGEST CHALLENGE BECAUSE THE CLAY SHIFTED DURING EXCAVATION AND THREATENED BUILDING FOUNDATIONS. FAR RIGHT: MUCH OF THE MINING WAS DONE BY HAND. WORKERS KNOWN AS SANDHOGS USED HAND AND POWER KNIVES TO CUT CLAY AND DROP IT INTO CARTS, WHICH WERE REMOVED BY MUCKERS. OFFICIALS AT FIRST CONSIDERED DUMPING THE CLAY INTO LAKE MICHIGAN TO BUILD A LAKE AIRPORT.

FAR LEFT: SUBWAY TUBE TAKES
SHAPE BEFORE REINFORCED
CONCRETE WALLS ARE ADDED.
CIRCULAR TUBES WERE USED
TO SUPPORT THE CLAY WALLS
WITH LINER PLATES AND STEEL
RIBS. NOT A SINGLE CAVE-IN
WAS REPORTED IN THREE YEARS
OF WORK. LEFT: TEMPORARY
TRACKS ARE USED TO MOVE
EQUIPMENT AND TOOLS AND
REMOVE MATERIAL.

THE MOST COMPLICATED PART OF SUBWAY CONSTRUCTION WAS RUNNING IT BENEATH THE CHICAGO RIVER. ABOVE: ENGINEERS BUILT A 200-FOOT, STEEL TWIN-TUBE SECTION ON DRY-DOCK ON THE SOUTH SIDE, AND THEN FLOATED IT INTO POSITION. WORKERS DUG A TRENCH ON THE RIVER BOTTOM, SUBMERGED THE TUBE, AND CONNECTED EACH END TO THE SUBWAY TUNNELS. LEFT: THE ROUTE OF THE SUBWAY WAS VISIBLE IN THE CHICAGO & NORTH WESTERN FREIGHT YARD, NORTH OF THE RIVER NEAR THE WABASH AVENUE BRIDGE.

FOR HOURS EACH DAY DONALD RAY RODE THEM: THE HOWARD, PAST ADDISON AND WRIGLEY FIELD, THEN BELMONT, THEN FULLERTON, THEN THE MOST EXCITING, THE MOST DAZZLING PART OF THE LINE: THE DESCENT INTO THE UNDERGROUND TUBE JUST PAST THE ARMITAGE STATION. IT WAS LIKE A MOUTH CONSUMING THEM ALL, CHANGING LIGHT INTO SHADOW AND DARKNESS, THE SOUND FROM A HUM INTO AN ECHOING THUNDER OF VIBRATION AND NOISE. ONCE BENEATH THE STREET, HE WOULD STUDY THE HOUSES AS THEY SLOWLY DRIFTED INTO THE LANDSCAPE; HE WAS SUDDENLY IN THE LEAD OF A LONG, CURLING MISSILE PROPELLING ITSELF THROUGH A HOLE UNDER THE EARTH, AND ONLY HE WAS IN CONTROL.

CITY DOGS BY WILLIAM BRASHLER

THE NORTH PORTAL OF THE STATE STREET SUBWAY IS FINISHED IN 1943 NEAR WILLOW STREET AND SHEFFIELD AVENUE. THE NORTH SIDE MAIN LINE'S "L" TRACKS ARE ABOVE.

S-1A
12-27-40
89

ABOVE: EMPLOYEES MEASURE STREET SETTLEMENT NEAR THE SUBWAY LINE AT CHICAGO AVENUE AND STATE STREET. THE FIRST SIGNS OF SETTLING WERE REPORTED ABOUT THREE MONTHS AFTER CONSTRUCTION BEGAN. DOZENS OF BUILDING AND HOME OWNERS, INCLUDING PROPRIETORS OF THE MONADNOCK BUILDING, SUED THE CITY. LEFT: SUBWAY STATIONS, CALLED MEZZANINES, WERE BUILT 18 FEET UNDERGROUND. FACILITIES LIKE THE ROOSEVELT AND STATE STATION WERE EXCAVATED FROM THE TOP AND THEN COVERED WITH A ROOF AND SOIL.

STATE STREET TOOK THE NAME "BURMA ROAD" DURING THE WAR BECAUSE IT WAS TORN UP MANY TIMES TO MAKE WAY FOR THE NEW STATIONS. FAR LEFT: DESPITE THE CONSTRUCTION OF STATIONS IN OPEN CUTS, STREET-CAR LINES AND BUS TRAFFIC ALONG STATE WERE KEPT RUN-NING DURING MUCH OF THE CONSTRUCTION. LEFT: TRAFFIC MOVES AROUND THE CONSTRUC-TION OF A STATION AT CHICAGO AVENUE AND STATE.

FAR LEFT: THE STATE STREET SUBWAY LINE OPENS TO THE PUBLIC. GIS WERE ALLOWED TO RIDE THE SYSTEM FOR FREE. BECAUSE OF A SHORTAGE OF MATERIALS, CONSTRUCTION ON THE DEARBORN LINE WAS HALTED IN 1942, EVEN THOUGH IT WAS NEARLY COMPLETE. LEFT: FOR SAFETY'S SAKE, ONLY STEEL CARS WERE ALLOWED TO RUN IN THE SUBWAY. THEY WERE ELEVATED TRAINS THAT WERE MODIFIED WITH EMERGENCY LIGHTING.

WHEN THE TRAIN PULLED SCREAMING INTO STATE STREET AND WASHINGTON BOULEVARD, HALF THE PASSENGERS STOOD AND FACED THE DOOR, SHUFFLING FORWARD IN THE AISLE. IT'S A KIND OF DESPERATE, GRASPING COMPULSION, YOU KNOW, STANDING AT THE DOOR LONG BEFORE THE TRAIN GETS INTO THE STATION— AS IF THE TRAIN WERE GOING TO GET THERE ANY QUICKER AND THEY WERE GOING TO GET OUT THE DOOR ANY SOONER.

ADAPTED FROM **COOLER BY THE LAKE** BY LARRY HEINEMANN

SOLDIERS EMERGE FROM THE STATE STREET STATION SOUTH OF ADAMS STREET TO A HEROES' WELCOME.

⭐ ONE FINE DAY ⭐

Charles E. Keevil was an equipment engineer who worked for the Chicago Rapid Transportation Company and the CTA. He was also an amateur photographer.

During the 1930s and '40s, Keevil was given several photo assignments by the company. In 1946, he photographed stations on every line—the Evanston, Skokie and Ravenswood lines up north; the Logan, Douglas and Garfield lines out west; the Kenwood, Jackson Park and Englewood lines down south, and the North Side Main line. In total, Keevil documented sixty-one stations, and life around these stations.

The photos here were all taken on August 1, 1946. They show Chicago's other underground, the shadowy land beneath elevated tracks. Keevil made prints for the transit company—some of which remain in the CTA archives. But he passed his negatives down to his nephew, Walter R. Keevil, who also works as an equipment engineer for the CTA.

"He never really talked about it," Walter said of his uncle's legacy. "To him, it was all in a day's work." ⭐

SOUTHPORT STATION ON
THE RAVENSWOOD LINE.

ABOVE: 58TH STREET STATION ON JACKSON PARK LINE. LEFT: CLOCKWISE FROM TOP LEFT, 51ST STREET STATION ON JACKSON PARK LINE, 14TH PLACE STATION ON DOUGLAS PARK LINE, KEDZIE AVENUE STATION ON GARFIELD PARK LINE, AND ADDISON STREET STATION ON RAVENSWOOD LINE.

⊱ THE NIGHTSHIFT ⊰

"I seldom put anybody off," the elderly driver of a Sheffield Avenue streetcar told reporter Ben Hecht as an owl car drove through the city. "The drunks are pretty sad and I feel sorry for them. They just flop over and I wake them up when it comes their time. Sometimes there's girls and they look pretty sad."

Travel through the city has always been different on the night owl lines. Connections are longer and the pace is slower as the third shift trudges home. It's a quiet world of empty seats and empty cars. Of small talk and laughter. Of buses that run early rather than late. Of trains being coupled and buses being lined up for tomorrow.

"Once there was a man whose picture I see in the papers the next day as having committed suicide," the driver said. "I remembered him in a minute. Well no, he didn't look like he was going to commit suicide. He just looked like all the other passengers—tired and sleepy and sort of down." ⊹

CHICAGO SURFACE LINES
SUPERVISOR AT HIS POST.

LEFT: CLYDE YOUNT REPAIRS A
SIGNAL AT ARMITAGE AVENUE.
FAR LEFT: STATE STREET AT
JACKSON BOULEVARD, LOOKING
NORTH.

167

BY ITS PADLOCKED POOLROOMS AND ITS NIGHTSHADE NEON, BY ITS CARBARN CHRISTS PUNCHING TRANSFERS ALL NIGHT LONG; BY ITS NUNS STUDYING GIN-FIZZ ADS IN THE ENGLEWOOD LOCAL, YOU SHALL KNOW CHICAGO.

BY NIGHTS WHEN THE YELLOW SALAMANDERS OF THE EL BEND ALL ONE WAY AND THE COLD RAIN RUNS WITH THE RED-LIT RAIN.

CHICAGO: CITY ON THE MAKE BY NELSON ALGREN

A LONELY SWITCHMAN STRADDLES THE THIRD-RAIL.

ABOVE: CONTROL INSPECTOR HARLAN HEIL FIXES A STREETCAR SWITCHBOX. LEFT: JAMES FINLEY GRINDS A WHEEL ON A GREEN HORNET STREETCAR AT THE KEDZIE CARBARN, KEDZIE AVENUE AT VAN BUREN STREET.

ABOVE: BUS DRIVER VINCE ANDREWS PICKS UP A RUN NUMBER TAG FOR AT THE ARCHER CARBARN, ARCHER AND ROCKWELL AVENUES. (PHOTOGRAPH BY THORVALD HAANIG.) LEFT: WELDING CREW CONNECTS RAIL ENDS. ONE HUNDRED MEN WORKED FULL TIME TO FIX BROKEN JOINTS ALONG CHICAGO SURFACE LINES' TRACKS.

❋ END OF THE LINE ❋

The Chicago Transit Authority inherited a fleet of 3,200 streetcars when it was established in 1947. A decade later, they were gone.

Like paleontologists, railfans yearn for the day when streetcars ruled the earth. But like dinosaurs, many of the city's streetcars were old and all of them lacked mobility.

The momentum to make streetcars extinct began after World War II, as buses were gaining in popularity. Public opinion turned in 1950, when the most modern of cars, a Green Hornet streamliner, failed to avoid an oncoming tanker truck loaded with 8,000 gallons of gasoline. Ghastly images filled the newspapers and fueled fears of being trapped aboard a burning streetcar.

"If the doors of public buildings must open outward, why not the doors of public conveyances?" asked a Chicago resident ten days after the crash. "I have noticed how impossible it would be for a person of normal size to squeeze thru the window openings of CTA buses. The new streetcars are metal caskets to all intents and purposes." ☩

FROM THEIR DEBUT IN THE 1930S, CHICAGO'S PCC STREETCARS WERE THE ROOMIEST, QUIETEST AND SMOOTHEST EVER PRODUCED IN THE UNITED STATES. CHICAGO BOASTED THE LARGEST FLEET OF THEM—BUT BECAUSE THEY RAN ON TRACKS AND COULDN'T MANEUVER THE ROAD, THEY HAD DIFFICULTY COMPETING WITH CARS AND BUSES. FOLLOWING PAGES: A GREEN HORNET AT THE OFF-STREET TURN-AROUND AT AUSTIN AVENUE AND MADISON STREET ON THE WESTERN EDGE OF THE CITY.

THIRTY-THREE PEOPLE WERE KILLED ON MAY 25, 1950, WHEN A STREETCAR STRUCK A GAS TRUCK IN THE 6200 BLOCK OF SOUTH STATE STREET. A FLAGMAN TRIED TO STOP THE STREETCAR FROM HEADING INTO A FLOODED VIADUCT, BUT THE STREETCAR OPERATOR MISSED THE SIGNAL AND HIT AN OPEN SWITCH AT FULL SPEED. THE DERAILED CAR SKIDDED INTO ONCOMING TRAFFIC AND PLOWED INTO THE TRUCK, WHICH BURST INTO FLAMES. MOST OF THOSE WHO DIED WERE CRUSHED AGAINST THE REAR DOORS AND INCINERATED. THIS IS THE SCENE TAKEN FROM THE CORNER OF STATE AND 63RD STREET JUST AFTER THE ACCIDENT. THE FIRE SET EVERY BUILDING ON THE BLOCK ON FIRE; SOME OF THEM COLLAPSED.

179

ONLY EIGHT YEARS LATER, THE GREEN HORNET MADE ITS FINAL TRIP ON THE STREETS OF CHICAGO. IN THE EARLY MORNING OF JUNE 21, 1958, ROOKIE CONDUCTOR WILLIAM E. RYE (LEFT) AND VETERAN MOTORMAN MARVIN H. MCFALL (RIGHT) PILOTED THE STREETCAR NORTHBOUND FROM 81ST AND HALSTED STREETS TO KINZIE AND CLARK STREETS.

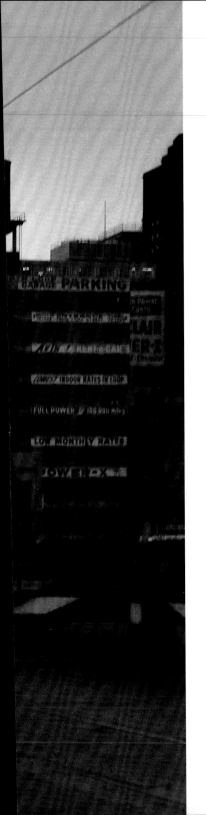

I COULD FEEL THE
MURDEROUS RUMBLE
OF MY DAD'S OLDSMOBILE
WEAVING IN AND OUT OF
NIGHT AND DAY TRAFFIC
LIKE A GULL IN THE WIND.
HE'D TOOL UP WESTERN AVENUE
AND REMIND ME THAT THE
GREEN HORNET STREETCARS
ONCE RODE THE LONGEST LINE
IN THE WORLD,
RIGHT HERE.

FROM **BUM TOWN** BY TONY FITZPATRICK

THE STREETCAR CROSSED THE DEAR-
BORN STREET BRIDGE OVER THE CHI-
CAGO RIVER, TURNED AROUND, AND
HEADED BACK SOUTH. AFTER THE
RUN, THE STREETCAR WAS TAKEN TO
THE 77TH DEPOT TO RETIRE. IT WAS
THE END OF WHAT WAS ONCE THE
LARGEST STREETCAR SYSTEM IN THE
WORLD.

❊ KING OF THE ROAD ❊

Buses were a late entry in Chicago. It wasn't until 1917 that the Chicago Motor Bus Company introduced double-deck buses along the lakefront and park boulevards. And it wasn't until 1927 that the Chicago Surface Lines debuted a small fleet of gas buses. That fleet grew to hundreds of gas and electric trolley buses by the time the CTA was established. In 1950, the new agency purchased 349 more trolley buses, and two years later added 595 diesel and gas buses when it bought the Motor Coach Company.

Through the years, the CTA has experimented with all sorts of ways to power buses, including the use of propane during the 1950s. Streetcar barns were transformed to bus barns as buses started substituting for streetcars on major lines.

"Approximately 298,000 daily riders on these lines are benefitting from the smooth-riding, rubber-tired, noise-proofed equipment, operated with less waiting time between vehicles," the CTA's *Transit News* boasted in 1954.

The substitutions were made permanent as the CTA covered streetcar tracks with a new layer of concrete or asphalt. The work, documented in photos, was called "street improvements." ✛

CEREMONY MARKS THE SUBSTITUTION OF TROLLEY BUSES FOR STREETCARS AND THE EXTENSION OF THE BELMONT BUS LINE WESTWARD FROM PACIFIC AVENUE TO CUMBERLAND AVENUE IN 1949.

ABOVE: CHICAGO MOTOR COACH BUSES ARE REPAINTED IN THE KEELER GARAGE, 4221 WEST DIVERSEY AVENUE, AFTER THE CTA PURCHASED THE COMPANY IN 1952. RIGHT: OPEN HOUSE AT THE NEW NORTH PARK BUS TERMINAL IN 1950. THE SERVICING CENTER, AT 3112 WEST FOSTER AVENUE, IS NOW ONE OF THE OLDEST BUS GARAGES. FOLLOWING PAGES: GREEN LIMOUSINES.

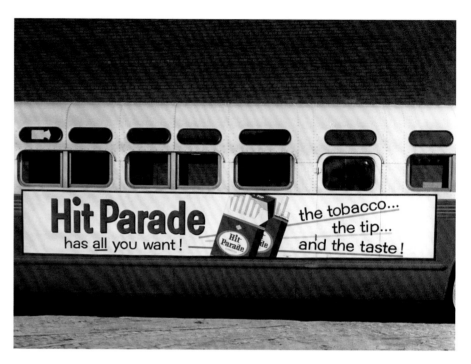

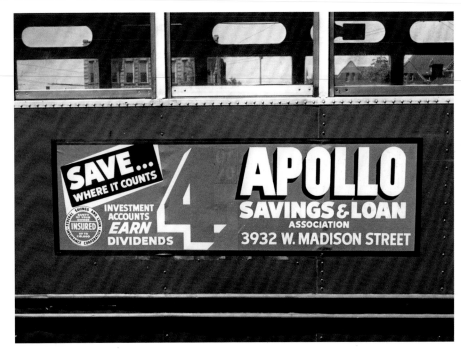

JUDITH AND DONALD REMKE ENJOY THEIR FIRST MOMENTS OF WEDDED BLISS ON A FLXIBLE TWIN COACH. THE COUPLE CHARTERED THE CTA BUS IN 1961 TO TRANSFER GUESTS FROM THEIR WEDDING AT ST. BASIL'S CHURCH ON WEST GARFIELD BOULEVARD TO A RECEPTION ON SOUTH DAMEN AVENUE. "I ALWAYS SAID MY DAUGHTER WAS GOING TO RIDE A BUS TO HER WEDDING," SAID THE BRIDE'S FATHER, CTA BUS REPAIR ASSISTANT FOREMAN ANTHONY KASMAN. "EVERYBODY THOUGHT I WAS KIDDING."

CHARTERS WERE MONEYMAKERS FOR THE CTA. ABOVE: MEMBERS OF THE EVANGELICAL LUTHERAN CHURCH OF THE REDEEMER BOW THEIR HEADS IN PRAYER AS THEY BEGIN A FIVE-COURSE PROGRESSIVE DINNER AT DIFFERENT HOMES IN EARLY 1958. (PHOTO BY THORVALD HAANIG.) LEFT: A GIRL SCOUT CHARTER TO EGGERS WOODS ON THE SOUTHEAST SIDE LATER THAT YEAR. (PHOTO BY ART TONNER.)

MAMA: YOU AIN'T SATISFIED OR PROUD OF NOTHING WE DONE. I MEAN THAT YOU HAD A HOME; THAT WE KEPT YOU OUT OF TROUBLE TILL YOU WAS GROWN; THAT YOU DON'T HAVE TO RIDE TO WORK ON THE BACK OF NOBODY'S STREET-CAR—YOU MY CHILDREN—BUT HOW DIFFERENT WE DONE BECOME.

A RAISIN IN THE SUN BY LORRAINE HANSBERRY

PASSENGERS PACK A BUS IN 1959. CITY STREETCARS, TRAINS AND BUS-ES WERE NEVER LEGALLY SEGREGAT-ED IN CHICAGO, BUT FEW BLACKS WORKED FOR THE CHICAGO SURFACE LINES, RAPID TRANSIT COMPANY OR CHICAGO MOTOR COACH COMPANY UNTIL THE 1940S. (PHOTO BY GAR FRANCIS.)

THERE WAS SOMETHING EXHILARATING AND UNSETTLING ABOUT GOING IN THE SAME DIRECTION WITH A MASS OF PEOPLE. WE GATHERED AT THE TOP OF THE ESCALATOR AND THEN ALL DESCENDED; WE WENT THROUGH SUNDRY REVOLVING BARS, WHICH PATTED US ON THE BACK, AS IF WE HAD JUST COME BACK FROM A DANGEROUS MISSION. IN THE URINE-SCENTED SHADE OF THE STATION, BUSES WERE LINED UP IN PERFECT PERSPECTIVE, SUCKING IN PASSENGERS THROUGH THE FRONT DOORS.

NOWHERE MAN BY ALEKSANDAR HEMON

IT WAS CALLED THE NIGHT OF A THOUSAND BUSES, BUT THE ACTUAL COUNT WAS CLOSER TO 800. IN 1954, THE CTA TRANSPORTED 38,400 PEOPLE TO SOLDIER FIELD FOR THE MARIAN YEAR MASS. AT THE TIME, IT WAS CONSIDERED THE LARGEST CHARTER IN BUS HISTORY.

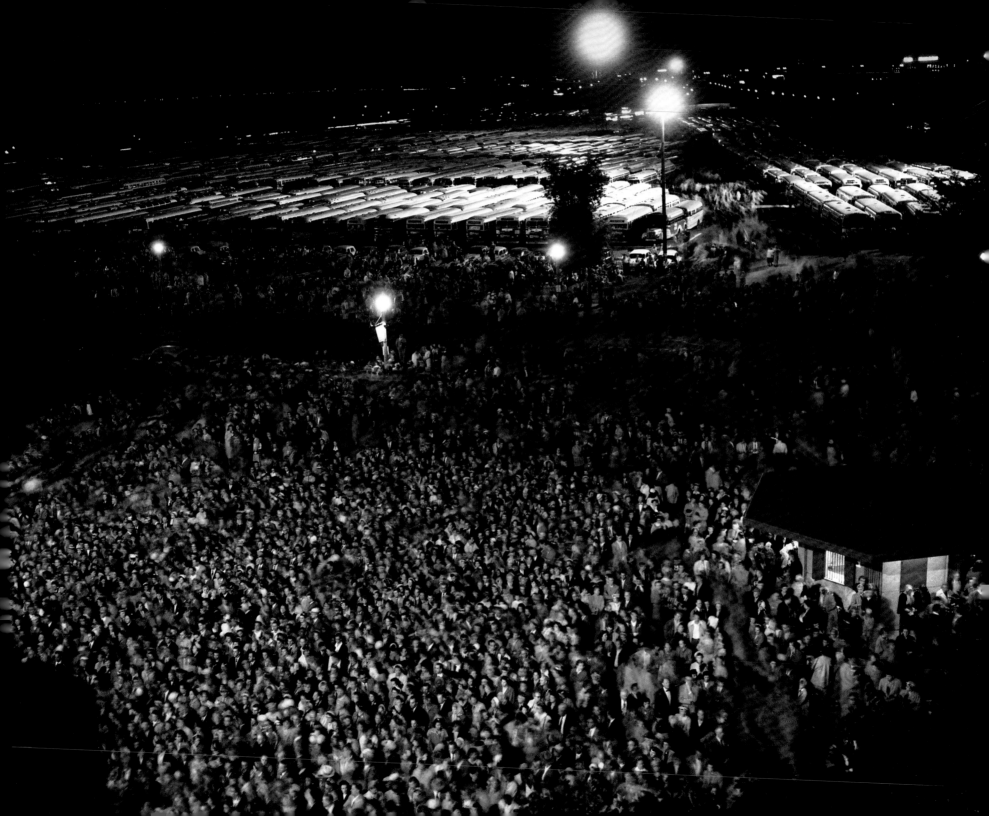

BUSES STARTED TO TAKE OVER THE LANDSCAPE OF CHICAGO AFTER WORLD WAR II. ABOVE: SOUTH SIDE FACTORY EMPLOYEES HEAD FOR TRANSPORTATION JUST EAST OF 119TH AND MORGAN STREETS. NEW BUSES STARTED SERVICE THERE IN 1946. LEFT: WORKERS LUBRICATE AND MAINTAIN TROLLEY LINES AT 59TH AT HALSTED STREETS. BOTH PHOTOS WERE TAKEN IN 1948.

ABOVE: A BUS TURN-AROUND AT 79TH AND HALSTED STREETS IN 1956. BUSES REPLACED STREETCARS THERE IN 1954. (PHOTO BY ART TONNER.) RIGHT: A TROLLEY BUS HEADS SOUTHEAST UNDER A VIADUCT ON GRAND AVENUE AT HOMAN IN 1953. STREETCAR TRACKS WERE COVERED OVER A FEW YEARS LATER.

ONLY A FEW DOWNTOWN STREET SEGMENTS DID NOT SPORT STREETCAR LINES. ABOVE: LOOKING WEST ON ADAMS STREET FROM WABASH AVENUE. LEFT: LOOKING WEST ON RANDOLPH STREET FROM THE ELEVATED STATION AT WABASH AVENUE. BOTH PHOTOS WERE TAKEN IN 1953. A SHORT LINE ON RANDOLPH IN FRONT OF MARSHALL FIELD'S WAS REMOVED AFTER WORLD WAR II.

❧ The New Look ❧

For ninety years, public transportation defined Chicago. By 1950, the city started to define public transportation. As Chicagoans moved to the suburbs and superhighways were built, existing rapid transit lines and surface routes began to lose ridership. To keep up with the changes, new rapid transit lines were run down expressway medians and some of the old lines were dismantled.

These were bittersweet years—an era that was unavoidable for a transit agency mandated by law to balance its books.

"Let us go back to the service we enjoyed for over fifty years, and to the ownership we once had, which tried to do its utmost to please the people, and with cheaper fares that were within our pocket books," lamented a Humboldt Park woman worried about the future of the Metropolitan's old Humboldt Park line.

Her line was closed a year later. And it was only the beginning. Throughout the next twenty-five years, new and old lines came and went as America became a car culture. Old buses and trains were traded in for "New Look" equipment. But for many, the old look could never be replaced. ✞

THE QUINTESSENTIAL CTA ELEVATED CAR WAS A MODEL KNOWN AS THE 6000-SERIES. THE MERCURY GREEN AND CROYDON CREAM CARS WITH A SWAMP HOLLY ORANGE STRIPE DEBUTED AT THE NORTH WATER STREET TERMINAL IN AUGUST 1950, AND BEGAN RUNNING ON THE LOGAN SQUARE LINE THE FOLLOWING MONTH. THEY WERE THE MAJOR WORKHORSES ON MOST ROUTES THROUGH THE 1980S.

RIGHT: MAYOR RICHARD J. DALEY WIELDS A SLEDGEHAMMER TO DRIVE IN THE CEREMONIAL FIRST SPIKE TO START CONSTRUCTION OF THE NEW CONGRESS RAPID TRANSIT LINE IN 1955 AT PULASKI ROAD. IT WAS THE FIRST RAPID TRANSIT LINE BUILT DOWN THE CENTER OF A HIGHWAY. (PHOTO BY ED EVENSON.) FAR RIGHT: THE NEW LINE, WHICH AT FIRST ENDED AT LARAMIE STREET ON THE WEST SIDE, CONNECTED TO THE LENGTHENED DEARBORN SUBWAY AT A PORTAL NEAR HALSTED STREET AND RAN UNDER THE CENTRAL BUSINESS DISTRICT. FOLLOWING PAGES: DURING CONSTRUCTION, THE GARFIELD PARK "L" HAD TO BE REROUTED AT STREET LEVEL FOR 2.5 MILES FROM SACRAMENTO AVENUE TO ABERDEEN STREET.

ABOVE: THE NEW CONGRESS LINE OPENED NEARLY THREE YEARS LATER, IN 1958, FOLLOWING A DEDICATION AT THE MORGAN STREET OVERPASS. THE METROPOLITAN'S GARFIELD PARK LINE, SEEN IN THE BACKGROUND, WAS ABANDONED BECAUSE THE TWO LINES FOLLOWED SIMILAR PATHS. (PHOTO BY J. EVANS.) RIGHT: THE HALSTED STREET STATION WAS AMONG THE FOURTEEN SPACE-AGE STATIONS ON THE NEW LINE. (PHOTO BY ED EVENSON.)

ABOVE: THE CTA COLLECTED MORE THAN $180,000 A YEAR FROM CONCESSIONS IN RAPID TRANSIT STATIONS, WHICH INCLUDED 268 GUM MACHINES, 267 WEIGHING SCALES, 145 PEANUT MACHINES AND TWO PHOTOMATIC BOOTHS. LEFT: THE SUBWAY ALSO CONNECTED TO MAJOR DEPARTMENT STORES.

213

TO DEARBORN ST.

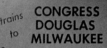

WEST-NORTHWEST trains to CONGRESS DOUGLAS MILWAUKEE

To visit Chicago is one thing, to live there another. This was not the Chicago of her vacations, where one is always escorted to the lake shore, to the Gold Coast, driven along the winding lanes of traffic of Lake Shore Drive in the shadow of beautiful apartment buildings, along State Street and Michigan Avenue to window-shop at least. And perhaps taken on an excursion on the lake. How is it she hadn't noticed the expression of the citizens, not the ones fluttering in and out of taxis, but the ones at bus stops, hopping like sparrows, shivering and peering anxiously for the next bus, and those descending wearily into the filthy bowels of the subway like the souls condemned to purgatory.

CARAMELO BY SANDRA CISNEROS

WITH THE TALK OF BOMB SHELTERS AND NUCLEAR WAR IN THE 1950S, SUBWAY STATIONS WERE VIEWED AS KEY URBAN BUNKERS. EVEN IF WAR NEVER CAME, THE SUBWAYS WERE A SHELTER FROM BITTER WINTERS. THE DEARBORN SUBWAY, DELAYED FOR YEARS, FINALLY OPENED IN 1951. IT CONNECTED TO THE NEW CONGRESS LINE SEVEN YEARS LATER.

LEFT: THE METROPOLITAN'S LOGAN SQUARE LINE WAS EXTENDED NORTHWEST UNDER LOGAN SQUARE AS A SUBWAY IN 1968, ENDING AT JEFFERSON PARK IN 1970. IT WAS EXTENDED AGAIN TO O'HARE INTERNATIONAL AIRPORT IN 1984. ABOVE: A NEW LINE DOWN THE MEDIAN OF THE DAN RYAN EXPRESSWAY TO 95TH STREET OPENED IN 1969. THIS STATION IS AT 69TH STREET.

INSTRUCTOR JOSEPH CHRISTY
SHOWS HOW A TROLLEY POLE IS
ADJUSTED. THE CTA RAN ITS LAST
TROLLEY BUSES——ALONG PU-
LASKI, CICERO AND NORTH——IN
1973.

"THE MOST UNUSUAL THING I EVER FOUND WAS A WOMAN'S GIRDLE," CONDUCTOR JAMES MCPHEE TOLD THE TRANSIT NEWS. "BEFORE TURNING IT IN, I WAS MODELING IT WITH MY MOTORMAN WHEN A LADY CAME INTO THE TRAIN ROOM AND SAW US AND GRABBED THE GIRDLE AND SAID, 'GIVE ME THAT, IT'S MINE.'"

CLOCKWISE, FROM TOP LEFT: IN-
FORMATION SUPERVISOR GEORGE
KELLY, CONDUCTOR FRANK ROB-
INSON, TICKET AGENT CATH-
ERINE COYNE, AND BUS CLEANER
WAYNE MIEDEMA. ASKED BY THE
TRANSIT NEWS HOW HE PLANNED
TO USE HIS CTA SAVINGS, MI-
EDEMA REPLIED: "NEXT YEAR
A VERY LUCKY GIRL IS GOING
TO LEAD ME TO THE ALTAR AND
THESE BONDS WILL MAKE A VERY
NICE NEST EGG."

CLOCKWISE, FROM TOP LEFT: CONDUCTOR GEORGE WOODMORE, PORTER STEPHEN CUNNINGHAM, PORTER O. BUCHANAN, AND MARY WALLACE, THE CTA'S FIRST WOMAN BUS DRIVER. WHEN ASKED ABOUT UNUSUAL FINDS, WOODMORE RESPONDED, "I HAD GONE ABOUT SIX MONTHS WITHOUT MY FALSE TEETH AND THEN I FOUND A SET ON THE TRAIN. THE NEXT DAY I GOT MY OWN FALSE TEETH AND EVERYONE THOUGHT I WAS WEARING THE ONES I FOUND."

OPERATOR JOSEPH GILIO: "WITH
WINTER DRIVING, ONE CAN'T BE
TOO CAUTIOUS."

A CONDUCTOR IN THE HAMLIN YARD ON THE LAKE STREET LINE IN WEST GARFIELD PARK IN 1958. FOR DECADES, TRAIN CONDUCTORS HAD TO STAND OUTSIDE BETWEEN TRAINS TO OPEN AND CLOSE DOORS.

THE LAWS THAT CREATED AND DEFINED THE CHICAGO TRANSIT AUTHORITY IN THE 1940S MANDATED THAT THE CTA STRIVE FOR MOD-
ERNIZATION. IN THE PROCESS, THE CTA CLOSED SEVERAL FACILITIES. ABOVE: THE LAKE STREET LINE'S ANCIENT MARKET STREET TRACK
IS TAKEN APART ABOVE WACKER DRIVE IN 1948. RIGHT: THE METROPOLITAN MAIN LINE, WHOSE TRACKS CROSSED DIRECTLY ATOP THE
UNION STATION TRAIN SHED, IS REMOVED IN 1961, YEARS AFTER THE LINE WAS ABANDONED.

BY THE 1960S, LITTLE WAS LEFT OF THE ORIGINAL METROPOLITAN'S LINES. RIGHT: SECTIONS OF THE LOGAN SQUARE BRANCH, A NORTH-SOUTH TRACK ALONG PAULINA AVENUE, WERE RAZED IN 1964. (PHOTO BY GAR FRANCIS.) FAR RIGHT: TEN YEARS EARLIER, THE METROPOLITAN'S TWO-MILE HUMBOLDT PARK LINE WAS RAZED. THE LINE, WHICH BRANCHED OFF AT THE DAMEN AVENUE STATION NEAR NORTH AVENUE, RAN STRAIGHT WEST TO LAWNDALE AVENUE. IT CLOSED IN 1952.

SOMETIMES WHEN I GET ON THE TRAIN I LEAN MY HEAD AGAINST THE WINDOW, CLOSE MY EYES AND LET MYSELF REMEMBER AGUSTÍN, WHO WAS NOT DARK LIKE MANOLO, BUT CREAM-COLORED LIKE VANILLA. . . . ON THE TRAIN RIDE HOME, SOMETIMES, NOT ALWAYS, I THINK OF AGUSTÍN AND HIS PALE GRAY EYES, SAD LIKE A RAIN CLOUD, AND BUSHY REDDISH-BLOND EYEBROWS, AND I SMILE MYSELF INTO A LITTLE NAP. SIX STOPS UNTIL I GET OFF, WITH LONG CLANKETY-CLANK TIME BETWEEN THEM.

PEEL MY LOVE LIKE AN ONION BY ANA CASTILLO

ELEVATED TRAINS BACK UP ON THE NORTH SIDE'S MAIN LINE ON A COLD WINTER DAY IN 1960. THE PHOTOGRAPH WAS TAKEN FROM THE SEVENTH FLOOR OF THE MERCHANDISE MART. THE CTA MOVED ITS MAIN HEAD-QUARTERS THERE IN 1953.

229

RIGHT: THE 43RD STREET STA-
TION IN 1962. THE STATION WAS
A LOCATION IN "THE STING,"
A 1973 FILM STARRING ROBERT
REDFORD AND PAUL NEWMAN.
IT WAS DESTROYED BY FIRE THE
FOLLOWING YEAR. FAR RIGHT: A
NORTH SHORE LINE ELECTROLIN-
ER PULLS INTO THE ROOSEVELT
ROAD STATION IN JANUARY 1963.
THE ELECTRIC INTERURBAN CON-
NECTED CHICAGO AND MILWAU-
KEE AND RAN ON CTA TRACKS IN
CHICAGO. IT SHUT DOWN TWO
DAYS AFTER THIS PICTURE WAS
TAKEN, A VICTIM OF NEWLY
OPENED EXPRESSWAYS.

THE NEW CTA DISCONTINUED
RAPID TRANSIT SERVICE ON THE
SKOKIE VALLEY LINE BETWEEN
HOWARD AND DEMPSTER STA-
TION IN 1948, BUT REINSTITUTED
IT IN 1964 AFTER THE INTERUR-
BAN CLOSED. THE SKOKIE SWIFT
AVERAGED SPEEDS OF CLOSE TO
50 MILES PER HOUR AND TOOK
THE TITLE AS THE WORLD'S FAST-
EST RAPID TRANSIT LINE. RIGHT:
SEVEN STATIONS ALONG THE
LINE WERE DEMOLISHED IN THE
1960S, INCLUDING THE KOSTNER
AVENUE STATION. FAR RIGHT:
THE SWIFT USED A SPECIAL AIR-
FOIL PANTAGRAPH, INVENTED IN
THE SKOKIE SHOPS, THAT GLIDED
ON OVERHEAD WIRE. (PHOTO BY
ART TONNER.)

WOOD RAPID TRANSIT CARS HAD A REMARKABLE RUN—MOST LASTED MORE THAN FIFTY YEARS. BUT BY LATE 1957, THEY WERE PHASED OUT. RIGHT: A TOWER-MAN DIRECTS WOOD AND STEEL CARS IN 1951. FAR RIGHT: WOOD CARS ARE BURNED IN THE SKOKIE YARDS IN 1960. THE CARS WERE SCRAPPED STARTING IN 1947. (PHOTO BY GAR FRANCIS.)

FAR LEFT: THE STATE AND LAKE STATION. THE STATION DATES BACK TO 1895, WHEN THE LAKE STREET ELEVATED FIRST EXTENDED ITS LINE TO THE NORTH END OF THE LOOP. IT IS THE OLDEST LOOP STATION. LEFT: THE LAKE AND CLARK STATION, WHICH WAS RE-PLACED BY A MODERN FACILITY IN THE EARLY 1990S. BOTH PICTURES WERE TAKEN IN 1961. (PHOTOS BY GAR FRANCIS.)

ABOVE: THE HOWARD STREET STATION, AT HERMITAGE AVENUE IN ROGERS PARK, IN 1963, JUST BEFORE IT WAS REMODELED. (PHOTO BY GAR FRANCIS.) LEFT: THE LAKE AND CLINTON STATION AT 540 WEST LAKE STREET IN 1966. (PHOTO BY ART TONNER.)

WILSON STATION, AT THE NORTHWEST CORNER OF WILSON AND BROADWAY, WAS BUILT AS A GRANDIOSE STATION IN THE THRIVING NEIGHBORHOOD OF UPTOWN IN 1923 FOR THE NORTHWESTERN ELEVATED AND NORTH SHORE LINE. BY THE TIME THE INTERURBAN CLOSED IN 1963, THE STATION'S WAITING ROOM HAD BEEN CONVERTED INTO A SHORT-ORDER RESTAURANT AND ARCADE.

MOST RAPID TRANSIT STATIONS ALONG THE ROUTE WERE LITTLE MORE THAN TICKET AGENT BOOTHS. IN 1997, AGENTS WERE PHASED OUT. LEFT: A LOOP STATION BOOTH ABOVE VAN BUREN STREET IN 1971. FAR LEFT: EVANSTON'S CENTRAL STREET STATION WAS THE END OF THE NORTHWESTERN LINE WHEN THE STATION, AT 1022 CENTRAL, OPENED IN 1908. THE STATION WAS OVERSIZED TO ALLOW FOR LARGE CROWDS ATTENDING FOOTBALL GAMES AT NEARBY NORTHWESTERN UNIVERSITY'S DYCHE STADIUM. (PHOTOGRAPH BY ART TONNER.)

RIGHT: THE NORTH LINE WAS PUSHED TO WILMETTE IN 1912, WHEN LINDEN STREET STATION BECAME THE NORTHERN TERMINAL. HERE STEEL CARS FROM DIFFERENT ERAS SUN THEMSELVES IN THE NEARBY YARD IN 1972. FAR RIGHT: FOR ALMOST A CENTURY, THE WILSON YARD AND SHOPS, SHOWN IN 1959 JUST SOUTH OF THE WILSON STATION, WAS THE MAJOR MAINTENANCE FACILITY FOR THE ELEVATED ON THE NORTH SIDE. THE SHOP BURNED TO THE GROUND IN AN EARLY MORNING FIRE IN 1996. (PHOTO BY GAR FRANCIS.)

WHERE MOONLIGHT ANGLES
      THROUGH THE EAST-WEST STREETS,
DOWN AMONG THE OLD
      FOR AMERICA
TALL BUILDINGS THAT CHANGED
      THE STREETS OF OTHER
CITIES CIRCULATE
      ELEVATED TRAINS
OVERHEAD SHRIEKING
      AND DRUMMING, LIT BY
EXPLOSIONS OF SPARKS
      THAT HARM NO ONE AND
THE SHADOWED PERSONS
      WALKING UNDERNEATH
THE ERRATIC WAVES
      NOT OF THE LAKE BUT
OF NOISE MOVE THROUGH FOG
      SIEVED BY THE STEEL MESH
OF THE SUPPORTING
      STRUCTURES OR THROUGH RAIN
THAT RINSES PAVEMENTS
      AND THE EL PLATFORMS
OR THROUGH NEW SNOW THAT
      QUIETS CORNERS, MOODS,
RIVETED CAREERS.

FROM TRAIN ABOVE PEDESTRIANS
BY REGINALD GIBBONS

THE 58TH STREET STATION, AT PRAIRIE AVENUE, IN 1972. THIS WAS ONE OF THE ORIGINAL STATIONS BUILT IN 1893 BY THE SOUTH SIDE RAPID TRANSIT COMPANY. THE HUMP-SHAPED CANOPIES WERE UNIQUE TO THE SOUTH SIDE STATIONS. NONE REMAIN TODAY.

CHICAGO'S RAPID TRANSIT COMPANIES DELIVERED FREIGHT FROM 1920 TO 1973. FREIGHT CARS WERE PICKED UP AT THE BUENA INTERCHANGE YARD NEAR THE SHERIDAN STATION, AND MOVED BY ELECTRIC LOCOMOTIVE USUALLY AT NIGHT. AS THE USE OF COAL PHASED OUT, SO WAS THE SERVICE. THESE PHOTOS SHOW CARL LYDAY USING A FUSEE FLARE TO COMMUNICATE WITH MOTORMAN JOHN GIFFORD NEAR THE LILL COAL AND OIL COMPANY, 1121 WEST BALMORAL AVENUE, IN 1965. (PHOTOS BY ART TONNER AND GAR FRANCIS.)

ABOVE: THE REMAINS OF THE NORTH WATER STREET TRACKS EXTEND EAST FROM THE MERCHANDISE MART STATION IN THIS VIEW FROM MARINA CITY. THE TRACKS WERE TORN DOWN SHORTLY AFTER THIS PICTURE WAS TAKEN IN 1963. RIGHT: A TICKET AGENT'S BOOTH AT THE LAKE AND CLINTON STATION IN 1966. (PHOTOS BY ART TONNER.)

LET'S MEET IN THE LOOP.

COME IN ON THE TRAIN THAT ONLY APPROXIMATES TIME, WITH A WOMAN'S MAGAZINE YOU'LL LEAVE BEHIND ON THE SEAT YOU HAD ALL TO YOUR OWN. INSTEAD OF READING, YOU'LL SAY YOU RODE TO A SONG IN YOUR MIND. (NIGHT AND DAY OR MAYBE MY FUNNY VALENTINE.)

WHILE, AT THE STATION, I'LL THINK I GLIMPSED YOUR OVERNIGHT BAG, THE ONE THAT LOOKS LIKE A REMNANT FROM A FLYING CARPET, DISAPPEARING INTO THE FRIDAY NIGHT CROWD RUSHING FROM WORK. DESPITE CELL PHONES, THEY SEEM CONNECTED ONLY BY GROUNDED CARRIER PIGEONS AND RECKLESS MESSENGERS ON BIKES.

IT'S FALL. LATER, THE L WILL CLATTER BY A SILENT HOTEL FULL OF THE STRANGERS WHO MAKE US EVEN MORE OURSELVES. BUT FOR NOW, I'M WATCHING THE WRONG TRACK, WAITING, BRACED AGAINST A COIN BOX FOR CRAIN'S BUSINESS NEWS. (MAYBE TIME ON MY HANDS OR I CONCENTRATE ON YOU.) YOU'LL COME UP BEHIND ME AND ASK, "ARE YOU LOST, LITTLE BOY?"

DON'T WORRY IT'S LATE; I'LL WAIT.

LOOP BY STUART DYBEK

LAKE AND CLINTON, STAIRWAY TO THE CITY. (PHOTO BY ART TONNER.)

POINTS OF INTEREST

FEATURED IN

CHICAGO

❖ CITY ON THE MOVE ❖

☞ *Find the many highlights of "THE CITY BEAUTIFUL" by using this handy free map! Numbers NEXT to the locations refer to page numbers IN the book.*

WARNING: *While this map is useful, its PRIMARY function is to help locate photographs featured in this book!* NOT AN OFFICIAL MAP 🖎

Office of CityFiles Press

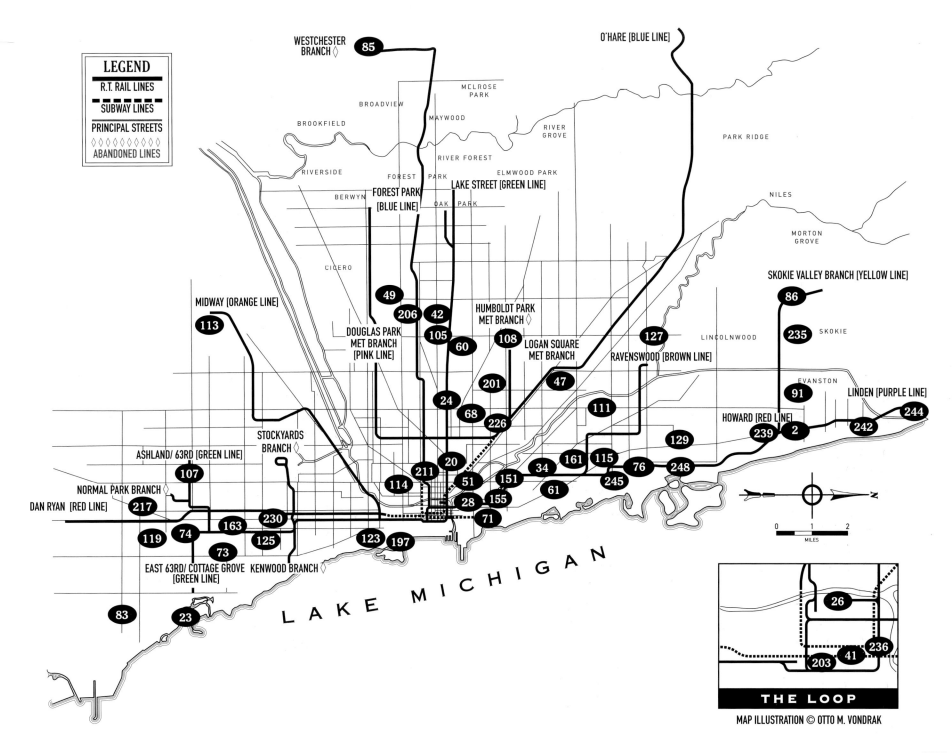

LEGEND
R.T. RAIL LINES
SUBWAY LINES
PRINCIPAL STREETS
ABANDONED LINES

WESTCHESTER BRANCH ◊ 85

O'HARE [BLUE LINE]

MELROSE PARK

BROADVIEW

BROOKFIELD

MAYWOOD

RIVER GROVE

PARK RIDGE

RIVERSIDE

RIVER FOREST

FOREST PARK

ELMWOOD PARK

NILES

BERWYN

OAK PARK

FOREST PARK [BLUE LINE]

LAKE STREET [GREEN LINE]

MORTON GROVE

CICERO

MIDWAY [ORANGE LINE]   113

49   206   42   105   60

DOUGLAS PARK MET BRANCH [PINK LINE]

HUMBOLDT PARK MET BRANCH ◊   108

SKOKIE VALLEY BRANCH [YELLOW LINE]   86

235   SKOKIE

LOGAN SQUARE MET BRANCH

127   LINCOLNWOOD

EVANSTON

201   47

RAVENSWOOD [BROWN LINE]

91

24   68   226

111

LINDEN [PURPLE LINE]   244

HOWARD [RED LINE]   239   2   242

STOCKYARDS BRANCH ◊

ASHLAND/ 63RD [GREEN LINE]   107

20   129

211   51   151   34   161   115   76   248

114   28   155   61   245

NORMAL PARK BRANCH ◊

DAN RYAN [RED LINE]   217

71

163   230

119   74   125   123   197

73

EAST 63RD/ COTTAGE GROVE [GREEN LINE]   KENWOOD BRANCH ◊

0   1   2   MILES

N

83   23

L A K E   M I C H I G A N

THE LOOP

26

203   41   236

MAP ILLUSTRATION © OTTO M. VONDRAK

255

ACKNOWLEDGMENTS

This book was built with a great deal of help and knowledge.

Supporting us at the CTA were Michael J. Shiffer, Cindy R. Kienzle, Joyce A. Shaw and Noelle Gaffney. The CTA granted us permission to study its photo archives, and gave us permission to use photographs—but in no way made suggestions or put restrictions on the book.

Assisting us with the accuracy and details of the photographs were life-long railfans Jeffrey L. Wien, Raymond DeGroote Jr., Eric Bronsky and Graham Garfield. Garfield's website, www.chicago-l.org, is the most helpful source of information on Chicago rapid transit history. We recommend it to those who want to better understand the city.

Helping us piece together the story of the archives and photographs were Robert Heinlein, Arthur H. Peterson, Roy Benedict, J. J. Sedelmaier, Malcolm D. McCarter, Scott Bernstein, David Phillips and Isaiah Williams Jr., one of the last CTA photographers.

We relied on the scholarship of many railfans, and hope this book adds to the rich literature on the subject. The bibles of Chicago transit history are *Chicago Surface Lines: An Illustrated History* (Transport History Press, 1974) by Alan R. Lind and *The "L": The Development of Chicago's Rapid Transit System, 1888-1932* (Central Electric Railfans' Association, 1995) by co-author Bruce Moffat.

And guiding us through the wonderful world of Chicago writing were Bill Savage, Kenan Heise, R. Craig Sautter—all valued customers of the fabled City-Files bookstore—as well as Carl Smith, Pam Weinberg, Sarah Conway, Susan Bergholz and Naomi Shihab Nye.

We want to give special thanks to Walter R. Keevil, who cheerfully let us paw through the wonderful collection of his uncle's negatives, and then trusted us to scan and return them. (We did.)

And for editing help, we relied as usual on Mark Jacob, Cate Cahan, Caleb Burroughs, Tim Samuelson and Karen Burke, valued supporters of all of our projects.

Finally, we are indebted to the Chicago History Museum, Skokie Public Library and Chicago Public Library, which helped connect us to 150 years of history, as well as the *Chicago Tribune* and *Chicago Sun-Times*, whose daily coverage of public transportation is so valuable. And finally, we thank the Chicago Transit Authority, which takes us and a million others around "The City Beautiful" every day, and (more important) get us home every night.

THE LAST WORD

We consulted hundreds of books, plays and periodicals about Chicago to find our favorite quotes on mass transportation. Our favorites, excerpted in this book, include:

If Christ Came to Chicago! by William T. Stead (Review of Reviews, 1894)
The Time Traveler's Wife By Audrey Niffenegger (MacAdam, Cage, 2003)
Neighborhood by Norbert Blei (Ellis Press, 1987)
The Jungle by Upton Sinclair (Doubleday, Page, 1905)
Another Way Home: The Tangled Roots of Race in One Chicago Family by Ronne Hartfield (The University of Chicago Press, 2004)
Knock on Any Door by Willard Motley (E. P. Dutton, 1947)
1001 Afternoons in Chicago by Ben Hecht (Pascal Covici, 1922)
Sister Carrie by Theodore Dreiser (Doubleday, Page, 1900)
Chicago Poems by Carl Sandburg (Henry Holt, 1916)
For the Love of Mike, More of the Best of Mike Royko (The University of Chicago Press, 2001)
Native Son by Richard Wright (Harper, 1940)
City Dogs by William Brashler (Harper & Row, 1976)
Cooler By the Lake by Larry Heinemann (Farrar, Straus and Giroux, 1992)
Chicago, City on the Make by Nelson Algren (Doubleday, 1951)
Bum Town by Tony Fitzpatrick (Tia Chucha, 2001)
A Raisin in the Sun by Lorraine Hansberry (Signet, 1961)
Nowhere Man by Aleksander Hemon (Nan A. Telese, 2002)
Caramelo by Sandra Cisneros (Alfred A. Knopf, 2002)
Peel My Love Like An Onion by Ana Castillo (Doubleday, 1999)
Train Above Pedestrians by Reginald Gibbons (Poetry magazine, June 2006)
Loop by Stuart Dybek (Stop Smiling magazine)